Love, Honor and Frustration

Love, Honor and Frustration

Allison Hughes

ZONDERVAN
PUBLISHING HOUSE
OF THE ZONDERVAN CORPORATION | GRAND RAPIDS MICHIGAN 49506

LOVE, HONOR AND FRUSTRATION

© 1977 by The Zondervan Corporation
Grand Rapids, Michigan

This edition 1979

Library of Congress Cataloging in Publication Data

Hughes, Allison.
  Love, honor, and frustration.

  Published in 1977 under title: Love, honor, and
obesity.
    1. Hughes, Allison.   2. Christian biography—
United States.   3. Depression, Mental
4. Corpulence—Psychological aspects.   I. Title.
BR1725.H77A35   1979   248'.2'0924   [B]   79-11909
  ISBN 0-310-26331-X

Printed in the United States of America.

There is a satisfied hunger when the spiritual dimension of one's being is alive and growing.

Chapter 1

I was having breakfast in my wide-armed, patio rocker, enjoying the sun on the south side of the house where I could soak up solar heat and read at the same time. My busy schedule had slowed to an occasional substitute teaching day and writing one children's book a year. Arthritis had something to do with my routine, but I never said so – out loud.

I noticed the mailman coming north along Birch Street. With this year's contracts duly witnessed and proofs returned, I wasn't expecting anything but slush mail. But old habits are hard to break, and I met him at the gate, little realizing that he was bringing me a voice out of the past.

I shuffled through a handful of periodicals in brown sleeves and fall catalogs in their bright full-color covers. Suddenly familiar words jumped at me from an envelope, as one's own handwriting does when seen unexpectedly. It was a printed mailing sticker, the kind I'd used years ago.

It was frayed at the corners and faded, but quite legible. Postmarked Shale Bay, Ontario, with a return address of Allison Hughes, R. R. 3, Georgian Sound, Ontario.

I swatted the envelope against the palm of my left hand speculatively. Eight years ago. Hmm, her children would be teen-agers now.

Gingerly I let myself down into my rocker and just as gingerly I opened the fat envelope. Several typed pages slid into my lap.

The letter began without salutation.

Mrs. Baker, I'm writing to you because somehow I think you'll believe me.

I tried to drown myself last night. I don't know why. I only know I was out there. Up to my ears in water. Cold, black, Georgian Bay water.

Nobody believes me.

I don't know what to do. Where to turn. I tried to explain to my husband, but he says to quit imagining things, that people will think I'm crazy. He thinks I had a nightmare.

But I know differently. I know I tried to kill myself. I don't know what to do. What can I do?

I'm afraid it'll happen again.

Suicide is ridiculous and stupid! I am so ashamed....

Suicide and Allison Hughes. The two just didn't go together. And yet they did.

My mind flashed back to the writers' conference eight years before when I had met Allison. I first saw her at the authors' autographing party, and I noticed her especially because she was different. She was young. And she was pretty. A willowy, golden-girl prettiness that stood out among the rest of us who were victims of secretary's spread – a common malady among not-so-young authors.

Most of the dozen or so authors, each sitting behind a

table piled hopefully high with his or her latest books, looked as if they had too little sunshine and not enough exercise.

But not her.

My curiosity prompted me to buy a copy of one of her several books on display. I read it in my room that night – right through to the last page. And I muttered as I read. "That's not the way life is! Only a princess in an ivory tower could write such fantasy and call it real-life Christian fiction."

I flipped to the back jacket to see where her castle was located and found she lived near Georgian Sound, Canada, was married, and had two children.

In that case, she must have met some of the realities of life during her twenty – no, thirty years. But you sure couldn't tell it from her writing. Her heroine, though alone, without money, and blocked at every turn, remained magically free from the frustrations of life such as fear, hate, anger, and grief. I found myself wondering about Allison. What was her marriage like?

I closed her book, flopped onto my stomach, tucked my arm under my pillow, and hoped that come morning she wouldn't ask me what I thought of her latest brainchild.

But she did. For in the course of a discussion the next day at the lunch table, during which we aired out personal views on Christian writing and what it really was and what it was meant to accomplish, my prejudice against church clichés and saintly synonyms in stories about pretty-pretty people came through loud and clear, prompting Allison to ask honestly, "You didn't like my book Lorna Hunter, did you?"

"I don't read much of that type," I said, stalling the inevitable.

"I do like a good romantic story with a happy ending. Romances, who-dun-its, why-dun-its, and other forms of

fantasy that make up the reading category I think of as
I-want-to-stop-thinking reading material." I knew my
big-mouthed honesty had my big foot right where it was in
danger of getting bitten again, but I couldn't stop now.

"Intelligent readers, as well as writers, know there are
two types of reading – the I-want-to-think and the I-want-
to-stop-thinking material. Often read by the same reader,
at different times, and under different stresses. Highly
intelligent and responsible people read and write the
stop-thinking material for legitimate reasons. I'm not
knocking it. It fills a real need."

"So why do I get the distinct feeling you don't like my
writing style?" Allison persisted.

I looked around and plunged in. "What bothers me
about your Lorna Hunter story is the fact that you are
writing in one category – take-me-away-from-my-problem
– and marketing it as the second type – this-is-our-world
kind of stuff.

"Allison, an acceptance of Christianity does not automatically make marriage a 'live happily ever afterward'
story."

She replied with sadness. "Mrs. Baker, you must be a
very unhappy person not to believe. . . ." There her words
dropped into silence, as if afraid further words would
inflict hurt to me, a bitter, old woman. And sweet person
that she was, I knew that she was vowing heavenward to
remember to pray for me. I loved her for that, and so I
opened my big mouth again.

"Allison, child, I am a much happier person now that
I no longer suffer from the good-little-girl syndrome. You
know how it goes – you be a good girl and you'll be happy
. . . all good things come to good people who wait. Believing such expressions as, you must live right, which implies God cares more for you when you're good.

"Allison, the millennium is not here yet. The lion still
roars; even worse, the lion eats the lambs. And good little

girls get hurt, deceived, swindled, even raped and murdered in this wicked old world.

"Writers, of all people, should recognize that 'do unto others as you would have them do unto you' is a command, not a promise."

Allison sighed. "I do realize that good people get hurt and die of cancer."

"And some become hateful husbands and lazy, slovenish wives, too."

She looked at me with those please-don't-wound-me eyes, so I added, "Scratch any seemingly happy marriage of ten years' standing, and you'll find it is only the continual forgiveness of Christ and renewal of the Holy Spirit that makes it any different from any marriage outside of Christ.

"The Christian marriage is just as problem-ridden as any other, if not more so."

Aunt Molly, another conference veteran, cut in. "Allison, you are married with two children. Have you lived this long and not known frustrations, anger, fear?"

"I suppose I would have, if I let myself. But – " she said the words as one would recite a pledge. "I am a Christian. I live by faith, not feelings."

This declaration seemed to wipe concern from her face, and she gave me a beautiful God's-in-His-heaven-all's-right-with-the-world smile.

I felt terribly sorry for her then and couldn't resist saying, "Someday your feelings may catch up with you, dear girl. I sincerely hope you have someone close to you who is willing to help you pick up the pieces and put it all together again."

Momentarily I had made her feel bad, and not knowing what else to do, I handed her a mailing sticker and added, "Write to me if you ever get the urge."

Now, eight years later, she had.

Chapter 2

Suicide is ridiculous and stupid. I am so ashamed....

Her letter continued, but now it lost its uneven impressions, its sense of incoherency. Her sentences became thoughtfully formed and completed.

Mrs. Baker, I had no intention whatsoever of doing anything so terrible. I just went for a walk. I often walk late at night when I am alone and the children are sleeping.

Grace and Jeremy, the children mentioned on the dust jacket of the Lorna Hunter book which you weren't happy about, are now sixteen and fourteen. Mark is almost eight, and Andrew is four.

When I go for a walk, our big black Labrador, Scout, sits on the back stoop, his ears tilted toward the open bedroom windows above him and his nose pointed down the road toward me.

Our village of Shale Bay is really only a horseshoe-shaped, graveled road looping off County Road 25, with the hoof outline filled with an odd assortment of homes amid maple bush. It's crescent-curved to the contour of the water, giving road access to the government dock at the bay. It is safe walking in our village at night, and I am never really beyond shouting distance from the children.

Now that I think of it, I've walked a lot this summer.

Yesterday my husband's sister Gladys and her husband Albert and their two boys, and some friends of theirs whom I'd never met before stopped in. The two families were on their way for a two-week trip along the St. Lawrence Seaway. Since Harvey was home having an early supper before going on the night shift, he asked them in for corn on the cob. The children and I had just finished husking sixteen dozen for the freezer.

After Harvey left for work, the two station wagon loads of supper company left for their holidaying. The children went to bed. Even Scout ate and settled himself for his summer-night sentinel on the clothesline stoop.

I was alone.

Often on nights like this, I am drawn toward the solitude of lapping water and the peacefulness of sitting on the wooden dock, still warm from the day's sun. Here I can stare out to sea with nothing to obstruct my view.

The whole night was at rest and unreal to me.

Neon lights from Georgian Sound across the bay were softened by mist and diffused into fuzzy fingers of color reaching into the water.

The normal sounds of some forty dwellings seemed eerie in the after-midnight stillness, as if magnified by the sense of emptiness in the village at night. The boathouses and private docks were deserted by daytime people — small children playing water games and teen-agers lying in the sun with transistor radios to their ears.

I sat in silence except for the slap, slap of small waves breaking against the dock and shore. With the end of the late news, the blue beam of TV tubes from undraped windows facing the water blinked out. A dog barked and was answered by another from up the shore road. A coon's call from some distant cornfield quavered on the early autumn air and died. The village slept.

Unkncwn to everyone, I sat at the end of the dock, arms wrapped tightly around my knees, rocking to the movement of the waves.

How long I was there I do not know.

At some point the serenity and beauty and loneliness of the night touched the deep aloneness within me. Tears came, splashing unbidden and undenied on my bare arms, dropping into the black water beneath me. I felt a oneness with the water. For it rolled toward me as steadily and relentlessly as my days — one wave so much like the next.

This summer had brought its own ceaseless circles of necessity. Each day I seemed to run faster and faster, until I was running as fast as I could just to stand still.

Tonight I was tired. Tired and alone. And I cried alone.

My reasoning mind said that a responsible, efficient woman doesn't cry. Another part of me wouldn't listen and cried all the more.

Here, alone on the dock, no longer mesmerized by my responsibilities or held up by my locked-in weariness, I unfolded my arms and slipped into the lullaby lapping of the water, to rest there, rocked between waves on the bay. Lifted and weightless, cradled there, away from urgency, demands, fatigue, and pain. I wished I didn't have to go back. Just to rock there. In and out, in and out. Each lapping carried me a little farther from shore.

My thinking mind said there was a sixty-foot-deep channel just beyond the shoreline shelf. But another part of me wanted to rock there forever, backward and forward, deeper and deeper.

Once when I bobbed to the surface, I heard a baby cry.

The children! I must go back to the children!

But my reasoning mind told me that was the Wynhurst's new baby waking for its 2 A.M. feeding. And an unknown part of me cried too, from a hunger I couldn't name.

As the rolling of the water grew stronger, I grew drowsier, and was only half aware that the strength in the rhythmic swell came from the channel tow.

Suddenly something strange and beautiful happened.

From somewhere too deep to know came the sound of words long forgotten in the busyness of living, in a voice long stilled in death.

"Tell me the story. . . ." It was my father's voice.

My father never sang in a chorus or a choir, but he loved to sing us endless verses about a frog's wedding, and another about a monkey that got drunk, and hundreds of hymns.

Now in memory I heard again his gentle, untrained voice singing so wistfully and so tenderly:

> *Tell me the story of Jesus, write on my heart every word.*
> *Tell me the story most precious, sweetest that ever was heard.*
> *Tell how the angels, in chorus, sang as they welcomed His birth,*
> *"Glory to God in the highest! Peace and good tidings to earth!"*

Peace . . . peace . . . peace. . . . The word seemed to come toward me like splinters of light on each wave.

Hand over hand I reached toward them. Peace . . . peace . . . peace. . . .

It was no use. I could no more hold the waves than I could hold peace in my daytime efforts. And I was too tired to try for either any more.

I let go, slipping downward through the chill water. Down . . . down . . . down. . . . I knew I was drowning. *I wanted to drown.*

Then the gentle voice came again:

Tell of the cross where they nailed Him, writhing in anguish and pain.
Tell of the grave where they laid Him.
Tell how He liveth again.
Love, in that story so tender, clearer than ever I see.
Stay, let me weep while you whisper. . . .

Daddy . . . daddy . . . daddy. . . .

Oh, Joanna, I weep even now as I write this to you.

Daddy . . . daddy . . . daddy. . . each call a gasp for air, reaching for strength I didn't have to keep from sinking exhausted into the depths of the channel.

Joanna, I am not a strong swimmer at best, but each time I broke the surface, the shore was a little closer — or so I believed.

Daddy, don't go. Daddy, sing to me a little longer. Just one more verse, daddy. My asking was an echo of a childish plea. Just one more verse, daddy, please.

Love, in the story so tender, clearer than ever I see.
Stay, let me weep while you whisper,
Love paid the ransom for me.

I was slipping back. I couldn't help myself.

O Lord, I cried. Lord?

And I tried once more. Chin touching my knees, I thrust with all the might I didn't have, clumsily jackknifing toward the surface again and again, until I flopped flat on my back.

With my head pointed dockward, my feet pumping, slowly I felt life begin to flow into my limbs. Ever so slowly I propelled myself toward shore.

After several efforts to emerge, I finally belly-flopped onto the wooden wharf and lay there, spread-eagle, drooling water, my arms and legs askew.

And the voice sang on:

Write on my heart every word.
Tell me the story most precious, sweetest that ever was heard.

Prostrate, in this nether world of nonreality, my mind gathered pictures around the strange sound of singing.

I had been upstairs in a farmhouse when my father sang to me that remembered time. He sat rocking me in a high-backed, wooden rocker.

Moisture filled that room, sending splintered shafts of colored light from a little oil lamp on an old-fashioned dresser not far from my head. The air was warm, steamy, and smelled of linseed poultices. I remember my mouth filled with the strong, gluey taste seeping through my swollen glands. Camphor-scented moisture ran in little rivulets down the misted mirror.

Father held me all that night. Wrapped in a blanket, I lay in his arms, sweat-soaked and feverish. They thought I was dying of a throat infection.

Over and over his voice sang softly through that night.

> Love, in the story so tender, clearer than ever I see.
> Stay let me weep while you whisper,
>   Love paid the ransom for me.

Daddy . . . daddy . . . daddy. . . . I grabbed the iron ring riveted to the dock. The feeling of drowning, of dying, of wanting to die washed over me again.

I hung on, lying flat, the lake rocking around me.

Daddy . . . daddy. . . . I survived the childhood illness. I grew up — a good girl. I went to Bible college. I trained. I worked. I followed the rules . . . daddy . . . I missed it . . . the peace. . . .

Like an echo through layers and layers of years came his words again.

> The cross where they nailed Him . . .
>   The grave where they laid Him . . .
> Love paid the ransom for me.

So why am I so alone?
Why do I weep?
Why did I try to drown myself?

*Here Allison's letter changed from the narrative style
to a personal letter again.*

Oh, Mrs. Baker, it was awful!

I am not a strong swimmer. That channel is deep
enough for lake freighters to navigate. If it hadn't been for
that strange remembrance. His voice came so strong, so
real, more real to me than anything else in that unreal
night.

I am so ashamed. So ashamed and afraid!

I go around the house questioning. Why? Why would
I do such an awful thing? I dread nightfall. I am afraid to
sleep, to let reality go. I'm afraid to go out the door at night.

Oh, Mrs. Baker . . . I'm writing to you for help, and
you've helped already. Just writing it out and looking at it
on paper, I can see the words and recognize them as the
truth, as one does a passage that is rewritten until it is a
true record of the known facts.

But when I say it out loud to Harvey, or the pastor, I see
in their eyes that they think it only the insane ideas of a
foolish woman or, at best, a nightmare.

Harvey put new locks on the doors in case the nightmare returns. He thinks the unfamiliar will confuse me
and waken me. The pastor of our village church suggested
I stop thinking about myself and get involved with other
people.

Mrs. Baker, thank you for being the kind of person I
can tell the truth to without apology.

*I smiled as I read the last few lines. The kind of person
. . . she probably saw me as a somewhat overweight,
middle-aged writer, with enough spiritual perception to
be an honest believer, yet critical enough of the fellowship
of believers to accept the strange and bitter tales that
sometimes come out of seemingly "Christian" situations.*

*I must write to her. No, the girl was desperate. I de-
cided to send her a night letter. I composed one then and
there.*

Evanston, Illinois
Friday, August 17

Dear Allison,
Your feelings are catching up with you. Don't fight
them. Explore them. Don't be surprised if it hurts. The only
way out of an ivory tower is *down*.
Attack your problem as the intelligent writer you are,
Allison.
1. Write out the drowning scene in full detail. Open
files, characterization, situation, setting, and theme, as
you would to begin a novel you are going to write to
incorporate the suicide scene.
2. Remember:

Life is real! Life is earnest!
And the grave is not its goal;
Dust thou art, to dust returnest,
Was *not* spoken of the soul.

Longfellow said it better than I could.
3. Read the Gospel of John, chapter 3, in every trans-
lation you can get your hands on, all the way back to the
original if possible. Read it as if you'd never seen it before.
Meditate on it.

I'll be praying for you,

Joanna

*Just so I wouldn't seem like the "answer lady" my
sons had sometimes accused me of being, I decided to
write a longer letter.*
*This was the beginning of a strange correspondence
that lasted several years, slowly unfolding an ever
stranger story – but all too common.*

Chapter 3

Several weeks went by, and I heard nothing from Allison. But hardly a day went by that I didn't think of her. I wondered if she was still alive.

Of course she was! The girl was a sincere, intelligent believer who. . . .

But if she had tried to commit suicide again. . . . In case of her. . . . There was no reason to notify me, a casual acquaintance at a conference, and one letter exchanged in eight years.

I decided to phone her.

With the receiver in my hand, I remembered how busy a young mother is getting children ready to return to school – clothes, shoes, jackets, lunches. And how difficult the one child who is left at home can be. In Allison's case, the one child left was the youngest of four children.

I decided not to phone and add one more personal demand on her time.

Yet I couldn't get her out of my mind. Here was a girl, a committed Christian, without terminal illness or any great outstanding debt, no alcoholic or narcotic addiction, yet she wanted to end her life.

She must be suffering from some deep sense of loss. Maybe even unrecognized by herself. So what hope had I of discovering it from this distance with my scant knowledge of her?

All I knew of her now was: 1) She tried to commit suicide. 2) Her husband thought it was only a bad dream.

Suppose it was just a dream? A girl with that frightening dream needs help and understanding!

"Not knowing has never stopped you before, mother." Echoes of my sons of yesteryear reached me. So naturally, I tried.

I wrote to her in more detail, some of the logical possibilities for her feelings projected from my concern for the Allison I'd seen at conference all of eight years ago now.

If it didn't meet her specific need, at least it would give her some sense of reality in knowing she wasn't utterly alone with her problem.

Evanston, Illinois
Saturday, September 8

Dear Allison,

Many people contemplate and even commit suicide, because, like Hemingway, they are unable to live up to certain expectations.

The unattainability of Utopia may be a pseudo-problem, but the suffering it causes is very real.

Even the expectations set before an individual in some church groups can be a utopian aim: e.g., be a Christian mother, Christian wife, Sunday school teacher, Christian Education Committee member, group worker, visitation, witnessing, choir. . . .

It all adds up to a colossal task, if not an outright impossibility. Yet to say so out loud can make you the "bad guy" in an assembly.

The popular mythology of "get married and live happily ever after" in church circles is another utopian aim of Western civilization. All the marriage manuals and self-help books, including those put out by the so-called Christian press, too often add to one's problem rather than offer any solution. At best, they are generalizations and rules: e.g., If you love each other enough, you can work it out and find happiness — if you are equally yoked together, or of the same faith, and obey the rules.

Logic will tell you several things.

1. Everyone has a different understanding of happiness.

2. Everyone has a different capacity for giving and receiving love, even a different understanding of love itself.

3. Faith, being an intangible, is difficult to evaluate.

4. Equal does not stay equal. Two spirits do not grow at the same rate in the same way, any more than two bodies do, even though fed with the same food and given the same exercise. Therefore, Christianity can actually add to the strain of a marriage relationship, because idealistically it requires cohabitation on a spiritual plane as well as physical and mental.

Therefore, the marriage relationship, at best, is problematic. Any hope of achieving the storybook or marriage-manual ideal, out of much less than ideal material, is an impossible dream.

If by some miracle it is attained momentarily, how long can it be sustained on the live-happily-ever-afterward level?

Then blame sets in.

This must sound terribly cynical to the girl who wrote the lovely-Lorna-type books, but consider it objectively.

Blame may never appear on the conscious level. Christians are noted for growing a supersweet crust to hold it in. But subconsciously blame breeds bad offspring — a feeling of being cheated.

A feeling of being cheated can usually be traced back to putting value on the wrong things. Thus when a marriage begins to go sour, we have such jabs as — she isn't what I thought she was. He isn't what he let me think he was. You don't . . . any more. You never . . . like you used to. Why don't . . .? When are you going to . . .? How come you never . . .? Why . . .? Why . . .? Why . . .?

Suicide is only the end of despair. Despair begins in a belief in one's own helplessness or worthlessness.

Continue to read John 3:16.

For *you* He, God the Father, gave His Son.

For *you* He, God the Son, gave His life.

Therefore, you are bought with a price. Therefore, glorify God in your body and in your spirit *which are God's* — divine ownership.

How can an intelligent person honestly contemplate worthlessness? So set to work. Set up research files to write the story of that suicide attempt. Gather only honest facts. Let your writer's analytical mind reach honest conclusions.

Continue to read John chapter 3. You are a believer — then believe! You will *not* perish. Let your mind dwell on that.

Do not contemplate the death of that which is dust. Think on the spirit. It will not die. Sing, read, talk out loud, do whatever you must to feed that imperishable part of you with its required imperishable food.

Think on verse 18. You are not condemned by God. Do not condemn yourself. Do not pick up feelings of condemnation from others. Face your own feelings honestly. If God does not condemn you, you have no right to condemn yourself to death.

Your own father sang it to you a long time ago.
Love paid the ransom for you.

Keep on singing this until you can sing it with joy and
know, even when you are not thinking about it, that you
are not condemned. The ransom is paid for you.

Research your story.

Keep me posted on your progress.

You are much in my thoughts and prayers.

Joanna

*As the letter fluttered silently into the mailbox and the
metal flap clanged shut behind it, I felt I'd sent an arrow
into the dark. Not that every word written wasn't the truth,
but it was general truth and, as such, limited in its help-
fulness to Allison's specific need – whatever that was.*

But I had reached out with what help I had.

*Walking slowly back from the street-corner mailbox,
scuffling through yellowed, fallen leaves, I smelled the
woodsy scents of maples in autumn and admitted to myself that I knew very little about Allison Hughes.*

*But I liked to think that my knowledge of life was
somewhat larger. Having once come down from an ivory
tower myself, I knew just how rough the way could be. And
I knew, too, that whatever hurt she suffered, there was
healing for her in the Holy Spirit. Healing for the subconscious. Healing for the soul.*

> *Saving my soul . . . is but the beginning.*
> *Making me whole . . . now that takes a little longer.*

Sometimes much longer.

Chapter 4

A month is a long time to wonder if one has said the wrong thing. Finally on a crisp, sunny day it came. A fat envelope with a clutch of Canadian postage on it that looked as if Allison had cleaned out her stamp box to reach the total needed.

Shale Bay, Ontario
Monday, October 8

Dear Joanna,

I can't thank you enough for your letter. I read and reread it like a drowning person clutching a log for buoyancy.

What you say sounds so sensible, so logical. *Sounds* is right too. I read aloud after the children are asleep upstairs. It takes the feeling of loneliness out of the house.

I've read John 3 at least fifty times this way. Many times during the day its phrases flash back to mind, and I mentally regurgitate.

Today is the Canadian Thanksgiving.

Harvey has the weekend off, the plant shut down for four days. He went to a flea market, in the Simcoe area, where men take old motors, car parts, and stuff to sell to the antique dealers and old car buffs or collectors of things.

The church is having a Bible Days program. Everything is Bible times — food, clothes, customs. The kids are having so much fun they don't know how much they're learning. My food list was easy today. Two large crocks of beans and one gallon of grape juice — I opted for Kool-Aid.

The program is one I wrote when I was secretary at First Christ Church on the Hill. I fashioned it after Klondike Days and Pioneer Christmas Party which are used as teaching aids in grade school history courses. I wrote the skits and routines back when I knew all the answers.

It is a big undertaking for our village church, and the pastor wasn't happy with me for not directing it, but I couldn't take on anything outside the home responsibility right now. I'm running so hard already that I sometimes think I'm spinning, losing touch with the ground.

So even though I feel guilty, sending the kids instead of going with them and working, I am happy about this one, big, beautiful day I have to myself. And it will go too fast.

Before five o'clock when the kids come home, I hope to write a rough draft to you from the pile of notes beside my typewriter.

Since thoughts never come to me at convenient times, I scribble them on tear sheets, which are the leftover blank pages torn from the children's scribblers at the end of the school year. These I cut in half and stack wherever I work during the day — kitchen, laundry, bedroom, living room. I even have a few blanks tucked behind the toilet paper rolls on the bathroom shelf. Thus whenever a thought hits me, I can jot it down, stuff it in my apron pocket, and when I get to my desk, which isn't until after the children are in bed at night, I unload my pockets onto my typing table.

This is the way I've collected materials for the novels I've written, stuffing files with notes for character, setting, situation, and theme. I found myself researching that girl at the dock in much the same way.

Thoughts never come to me in any usable order either. But with loose notes, I don't have to cut, splice, or retype, I just shuffle them around, shifting the first to the last, trying them every-which-way until some shape begins to show. Then I clip the stuff that belongs together as one unit with a metal clamp. When it develops into an understandable order, I write the first draft.

From my several weeks of notes I will write my First Epistle to Joanna.

Writing the most dramatic scene first is a good writer's technique. It simplifies one's thinking. But in this case, it was the *only* thing I had.

To write the suicide scene with full details I sat at my desk, closed my eyes, and typed as fast as I could. Rat-a-tat-tat-tat. The sound of my machine filled the emptiness of the house. When I reread that desperate cry for help I sent to you, the sight of the words on paper shocked me. Even reading it silently while sitting in the room by myself, I blush. Heat flushes my face, spreading to my throat and ears.

Joanna, no matter how many times I probe that memory, I still have no idea *why!*

The only thing I have to go on is the *who.*

CHARACTER: *She stood ear-high in the water. She didn't know why.*

Now that's some bright character. Only it's not funny ha-ha, it's funny-sad.

Would you believe, I actually spent three hours at the typewriter one night trying to characterize that person in the water? And I could only manage to do so in odd, disjointed ways. For example:

APPETITE: *Her favorite vegetable is cauliflower, served with a cream sauce.*

Joanna, I stared at the words, knowing I haven't eaten cauliflower for years. If I like it enough to remember it as my favorite vegetable, why haven't I had it? I'm the cook.

DRESS: *Her preference runs to tailored clothes, basic colors, with flair added in the accessories, a silver belt, a bright scarf. Using leathers in shoes, handbag, briefcase, and collapsible umbrella.*

Now whatever made me think of that? I haven't had an umbrella since I got married. I lost mine on my honeymoon. Nor do I have any smartly tailored clothes — at least none that fit me any more.

GOAL: *To write a children's story that Walt Disney Productions would make into a film.*

That's pretty dumb too. I haven't written a children's story for ten years, so how could I have that for a goal?

Note-making on myself adds up to nothing, except fuzzy, circular thinking that goes nowhere. Joanna, you called me an intelligent writer. Right now I doubt the intelligent part.

But I do have a shelf of books with my picture on the dust jackets attesting to the fact that I was a published writer once upon a time. So, as a writer, when nothing adds up, yet you know there is a story, it's back to the research.

From writing for the church take-home papers, I've learned that characterization for a biography is more difficult than for fiction — less flexibility. But this, *characterization of oneself,* has got to be the most difficult thing I've ever done!

But do it I must, for sanity's sake.

So I collected several more pocketfuls of notes. But the more notes I made the more confused I became.

At 8:00 P.M. one evening I typed at the top of a page —

NAME: *Allison Bender Hughes*

At 11:00 P.M. I had a neat row of headings typed down the left-hand side of the page: appearance, expression, gestures, mannerisms, habits of thought, negative, positive . . . and so on.

But all the fill-in areas on the right side of the sheet were blank. So was my mind.

Had it been a fill-in questionnaire about any other member of the family — Harvey, Grace, Jeremy, Mark, Andrew — I could have finished it in short order. But about myself — I was at a complete loss.

Joanna, I remember that a change of viewpoint can sometimes save a rejected story from File 13.

But I had only one character. The only change possible would be to the objective viewpoint.

Thinking objectively about oneself is a new concept for me. I found it takes time to develop an awareness of oneself after seventeen years of marriage — especially with five other people to think of first plus my Bible college training which stressed functioning on faith, not feelings.

The only method I could come up with was to try to catch myself unawares, as I would with a child shielding a secret hurt.

At first I felt silly watching myself as I would an incompetent. Yet when one of the kids suddenly bursts into tears, I automatically touch the back of my hand to his or her forehead for a quick temperature reading, and act accordingly.

When Scout trotted across the yard on a three-legged limp, I set down the potato fork I was using to dig supper vegetables and examined his upheld paw.

As I watched Scout race after Mark's bicycle, then looked at the thorn I'd extracted from his paw, I asked myself — "Silly as it feels, why shouldn't I examine myself for hidden hurt? I do for the children. I do for the dog! Am I not of more value than a dog?"

I am one of the "loved ones" of John 3:16. I am one whom the "beloved Son" came to seek.

You see, Joanna, all that reading of John 3 has sunk deeply into my soul.

Bless you, child. I looked up from her letter. Allison seemed a long way from finding the deep root of worthlessness she felt, yet she had found some sense of worth — at least as much as the dog.

Now wouldn't last month's after-dinner speaker at the Business and Professional Women's Club have fun with Allison's letter? She'd have to redo her graph and charts showing the horizontal strata of society so designed to place men at the top, then women, then children — economically, culturally, ecclesiastically.

Here was a Christian home structured with man at the top, then the children, then the dog, then the woman.

Whether real or imagined, that's the situation that seemed to come through to Allison, the woman involved.

There was more, so I read on.

Jeremy says I operate the home by ear. One time the south end of the house seemed too silent to me. I noticed it first in the morning while lying in bed, stalling for a few more minutes rest before starting the day's run.

Midmorning, when I paused for a moment at the dining room window where the sun comes in on cold winter mornings, I felt the steady silence but didn't bother to investigate.

When I opened the freezer door to get vegetables for supper, I noticed the light out. The freezer was unplugged, its cord dangling from a hook. And the makeshift outdoor light the kids and their friends used to light the pathway to the bay for night skating was plugged into the other half of the double wall socket.

They had pulled the wrong plug the night before!

Another time I mentioned to the children at supper — "Isn't that the sump pump starting up? There can't be water in the basement in August!"

There was. Harvey had turned the tap on to fill the laundry tub to patch the tractor tube the kids played with at the lake. He'd gone upstairs to shave while it filled, then went to work and forgot it. The well was sucking sand through the bottom foot feed when I caught it.

So I've learned to operate the house by ear, even more than Jeremy guesses. I can tell by the spatter of gravel on the driveway as Harvey's car turns into the yard more things than Jeremy knows about. As I can tell by the quietness of the screen door closing behind my oldest son at the end of his paper route just how bad his day had been.

So, Joanna, I am now listening to myself.

It sounds so strange, like listening to a seven-second delay of one's own voice at a radio interview, or the rerun of a speech in elocution class.

My choice of words is correct. I finish my sentences properly. Probably a hangover from speaking to women's groups, youth rallies, and would-be writers in the days when my books were still on the market.

Each day my voice begins its patient repetitions — "Quiet, children, daddy worked last night. Shh, your father is sleeping. Don't bang the door. Pick up your schoolbooks. Turn down the T.V. Children, please?" And it ends in a desperate pleading whisper — "Please, children."

As the evening wears on, I find my story-telling voice takes over, reaching a cheerfulness worthy of the line "they got married and lived happily ever after."

Then the iron kettle clamps on my cranium, and I can't hear anything for the pain pulling my head backward at the base of my neck. Except, of course, a monotonous drumbeat that grows louder as the pain tightens.

I've heard that pounding before. I stopped midway in my rush to the bathroom to listen. The drumbeats stopped too. Andrew screamed with glee. Water trickled under the bathroom door. I rushed to rescue Andrew from the tidal wave he'd created. Or maybe it was to rescue the bathroom from Andrew.

The drumbeats began again. I looked down. The pounding I heard, Joanna, was the sound of my own hurrying footsteps.

No wonder I feel as if I am running as hard as I can.

I am! In running shoes!

With Andrew looked after, I took the time then to look at myself. Really look at myself — head to toe, or rather toe to head.

White wool athletic socks and running shoes.

Harvey likes wool socks in his work boots. With so much synthetic on the market, it is increasingly difficult to find wool work socks. One day I found these on sale, so I bought six pairs, before I found out that Harvey doesn't like *white* wool socks.

Rather than admit I'd bought six pairs and run the risk of a lecture on my stupidity, I put the socks in my drawer. I've been wearing them bunched up in my running shoes for years. I don't think they're ever going to wear out.

Jeans, a too-small T-shirt of Harvey's, and an old work shirt with the sleeves cut off completed my outfit.

Joanna, I know that patched and put-together is *in* in teen fashions, but I was ragged, put-together ugly. I stared at the ugly image of myself until the tears started to flow and I could admit to the mirror — "Allison, you're a lardy old lady in leftovers."

I needed a haircut and set. I hadn't even shaved my legs for years. Why should I? The only dress hose in my drawer were dark-colored, with black seams up the back! I checked out the rest of my clothes in the three bottom drawers of our dresser and one quarter of the closet. Everything was stretched, shabby, left over from other people or another era. How disgusting! How did I get this way?

What way? A lardy old lady in leftovers!

So now, Joanna, I've added the household mirrors to my tools of self-characterization, looking at myself from the outside in I guess you'd call it.

Joanna, I never thought of myself as a pushy female. I've always abhorred such. But when I am not actually running, I push ahead, my shoulders thrust forward carrying a load of clothes, handing out school lunches, wiping crumbs from the table. Always reaching, stacking, baking, cleaning, peeling, washing, ironing, sorting, hanging up, taking down, picking up, putting away.

I look in the mirror. The face that stares back at me is my mother's — or so it seems for all of four seconds.

How awful! Not my mother's looks. She was a good-looking woman *for her age*. She was forty-one years older than I am now when she passed away last summer.

The image in the mirror goes watery before my eyes, but I stare all the same — head to toe, face, hair, neck, shoulders, arms, bosom, waist, hips, thighs, knees, calves, ankles, feet.

Oh, Joanna, you wouldn't recognize me, any more than I can recognize myself.

That awful sinking sensation of drowning washes over me. Only this time I recognize it for what it is — the suffocation of personal failure. I've got to do something. Now!

But there's no time. Harvey's car came in the driveway then, and he shouted, "How about breakfast for a hungry man?"

I promised myself, "Later. I'll face that mirror later."

Later when Harvey was asleep, the children in school, I stood in the kitchen amid the clutter of last night's bedtime snacks, that morning's breakfast and lunch-making, and Mark's speller. . . .

I've told that boy a hundred times not to forget that speller . . . will that boy never learn. . . ?

Suddenly I felt a terrible scream rising from deep within me. I choked to keep from releasing it. Harvey was sleeping, so I swallowed the bitter taste of it and turned my back on the messy kitchen and walked out. I closed the door quietly.

Andrew and Scout caught sight of me and scrambled out of their apple-tree fort to follow. "Hey, wait for me!" Eagerly he stuffed his little-boy hand in mine.

I walked this way with my father often. We used to tramp the bush on spring evenings, looking for a cow strayed into the deeper bush to calve. How sheltered I'd felt then, not caring if darkness overtook us when my child's hand was in my father's big farmer hand.

"Where are you going?" Andy asked, bringing me back to the present.

"Nowhere."

His surprise bordered on fear. "You never go *nowhere,* mother. Why are you going nowhere?"

Quickly I hunched down to face his concern eye-to-eye. "I'm going for a walk to see something beautiful."

I couldn't really blame the boy for the incredulity on his face, so with tension-draining honesty, I added, "Son, I'm sick of the sight of dirty dishes, dirty clothes, and unmade beds — and myself. Want to help me look for something pretty?"

Instant glee replaced his misgivings. He snatched a pebble from the graveled roadway and held it out to me, a crystalline chip of quartz flashed in the sunlight. I took his hand in mine and we walked at his four-year-old pace toward the bay.

"See how pretty the leaves are this time of year?"

He tipped his tousled head to gaze upward toward the

maple bush ablaze with red. The sumacs waved crimson seed flares against dark-green jack pines. The tamaracks lifted feathery yellow fronds to sweeten the autumn air.

Andy skipped and bobbed, ducking to pick a fistful of yellow-centered wild asters from the roadside. "Pretty?"

"Very pretty," I agreed.

Little white-capped waves bobbed and bowed in the morning breeze. I looked across the bay to the hills shining purple in October mists, and I sang.

> *Into the heart of Jesus*
> *Deeper and deeper I go,*
> *Seeking to know the reason*
> *Why He should love me so —*
> *Why He should stoop to lift me*
> *Up from the miry clay,*
> *Saving my soul, making me whole,*
> *Though I had wandered away.*

Andrew smiled, pushed his little body closer to mine, and said, "I never heard you sing 'fore, mummy. Sing more."

Oh, the poor child. How awful! I used to sing to the older children. What's happened to me, Joanna? What an ugly person this youngest child of mine has for a mother!

We sat for a long time, and I sang to my child. All the while my other mind raced about searching somewhere, everywhere for some idea of how I got this way. A harried, rushed woman who never goes *nowhere*, never sings. Always pushing ahead, giving orders: do this . . . don't do that . . . come here . . . go there . . . why did you . . . why didn't you. . . . Even in the quieter moments with the children I cut their toenails, trim their hair, check their school projects, hear their prayers. Doing, doing, doing.

Joanna, I can't characterize that girl at the dock. She seems like some distant cousin whom I haven't met since childhood.

I went to college, was taught what to do — deportment — and why — doctrine. I went on to study Christian journalism and was taught how to communicate the what and the why to the whosoever. But I lost touch with that child I used to be. I am now some unfamiliar, distant cousin to her.

I became a summer missionary, a church secretary, a director of Christian education, a writer. I knew life's answers, or thought I did, and put a lot of words into print to that effect.

Maybe I even helped some.

I became a bride, a wife, a mother — four times — a housekeeper, gardener, painter, decorator, cook, washerwoman, buyer, bookkeeper, judge, jury, garbage collector, and gravedigger for deceased pets.

But I don't know the answers. I don't even know the questions any more. Myself I cannot help.

After Andrew was born, I tried again to talk to Harvey about my feeling of aloneness. But he just echoed my question through clamped lips — "Who are you?"

Even before he answered, I knew I shouldn't have asked.

"I'll tell you who you are. You are my wife! Mrs. Harvey Hughes. And I wish you'd act a little more like it and cut out this foolishness. Reading and questioning and looking for highfalutin' answers to high-and-mighty questions. You're married to a working man — not a doctor or a lawyer."

"Oh, Harvey. I know I'm your wife. I have four children. I work fourteen to sixteen hours a day, seven days a week, fifty-two weeks of the year — "

"Don't start that holiday wrangling again. I work shift work, five days a week, and I don't want to go traipsing all over the country, lallygagging here and lallygagging there, looking for reasons to spend money for what isn't bread!"

Joanna, I remember every word so well. I was tired from nightly baby feedings and discouraged by the sameness of each day — dishes, diapers, clothes, and childcare.

"I'm a person, too!" I cried out. "Must I serve everybody else forever? Can't I ever be me?"

"What did you expect from marriage?" Harvey had never shouted at me like that before. "When a woman marries, she should be prepared to give her life to her husband, her home, and her family. Go read the vows you took! Go read that book on Christian marriage. You'll see!"

So I read the marriage vows I'd taken — to love, honor, and obey.

And I read that book, *The Home, Courtship, Marriage and Children,* written by a well-known preacher. It said everything Harvey said.

Joanna, Joanna, I tried all the rules for a successful Christian marriage all over again, for three more years.

Then I walked to the dock.

Try as I might, Joanna, I cannot characterize that girl who tried to drown herself, because I don't know her.

I am a stranger to myself. I've role-played so long that I can't find the real me any more.

Even when I don't go near the water, I feel as if I'm drowning.

Help!

Chapter 5

I refolded Allison's letter slowly, relishing a sense of relief. As much as one can deduct from this distance, she seemed safe from suicide for a while. Worried as she was, she had some renewed sense of God's love – enough to raise her self-evaluation to par with the family dog.

I would write her on the weekend, my usual letter-writing time to my sons Tim and Steve and others.

Evanston, Illinois
Sunday, October 14

Dear Allison,

Congratulations! You've made an astute assessment. You've role-played until you can't find the real you.

Role-playing is the line of least resistance. But the role isn't right if you can't feel good about yourself. Good about yourself in your relationship to the people in your present situation — especially those for whom you feel responsible.

The Fundamentalists' three steps to the successful Christian life are get saved, get baptized, and get to work, and they lead some to deduct that the more one works the more "spiritual" one is. Some even conclude that once saved, baptized, and working, the earnest Christian will stay on the top rung and hold the fort — where else is there to go?

Because such thinking, though as false as the idea that a good housekeeper makes a good mother, is subliminal, it goes unchallenged. When challenged, it is difficult to discern under stress because of the real relationship there is between work and spirituality, and between housekeeping and mothering.

It has been my experience that once the tangible becomes more important than the intangible, in either the home or church, growth of human personality stops or divides into offshoots.

Find a cow pasture to walk in if you have to, but find that happy child that hunted the bush with her father for new-born calves. Her personality is within you, maybe heavily submerged by the roles you've played, but there nonetheless!

There is much good literature in the public library these days on neurosis. Don't let the word scare you. *It is simply being what one is not in order to get what doesn't exist.*

It's the pitfall of all humans, this developing of substitute needs when real needs aren't met — and quite common among those playing a role unreal to themselves.

Keep on making notes. Keep on stuffing those files. Your true characterization and an honest understanding of it will emerge — though it may come slowly.

I'm looking forward to your next Epistle to Joanna.

Praying always,

Joanna

Chapter 6

Shale Bay, Ontario
Thursday, November 1

The Third Epistle to Joanna.

Greetings to my accomplice in survival.

This is how I think of you, Joanna. I have read several psychology books since last writing you, so my buoyancy material is growing. I read that many consider suicide the act of a mental case, unworthy of intelligent discussion. Many consider it a sin, unworthy of intelligent discussion. My husband considers it both, and thus unworthy of a moment's notice. But there is much, much more helpful data too.

Always in the back of my mind is the haunting question, "Why did I try such a stupid stunt as suicide?" I don't know yet, but in all of my reading, running, listening, and watching I am beginning to develop some awareness of me.

43

I find myself surprised by a sudden remembrance of things long forgotten. Sometimes it's only a vague feeling. Or an outline of something. Or a scent that reminds me of an incident long lost under layers of living.

Since the trend in some schools of psychology is to blame everything on one's childhood, that is where I started my self-questioning.

An unhappy childhood? Some traumatic experience? Misunderstood by parents? Mistreated by siblings?

I don't remember feeling hurt or unhappy.

I do remember the misery of some childhood tasks. The backache of carrying in firewood. The nausea of butchering odors at sausage-making time. The deadness in water-puckered fingers after peeling vegetables, especially tomatoes scalded for canning.

But I loved to fork hay, shock grain, pick apples, and gather grapes.

Mistreated by siblings? Often as not, I contrived to swap the jobs I hated to my sister for the ones I preferred. When I couldn't wriggle out of such household chores as dusting and scrubbing, I did them with such gusto that my mother gave them to one of my sisters next time. She couldn't stand the unladylike way I did housework.

Deprived?

I never had any money or any store-bought clothes except shoes and machine-ribbed, brown stockings. No store-bought cookies and bread like the town kids had in their school lunches. But I remember winter afternoons, walking the two miles home from school through roads unplowed, opening the kitchen door to smell apples baking in the oven, fresh bread cooling on the sideboard, and home-grown steaks simmering in an iron skillet on the back of the big wood stove.

Misunderstood by parents?

I don't think my parents understood me. But I don't think I wanted them to. For I had a secret world of my own where I wasn't just John's girl or one of May's girls — depending on which family reunion we were at.

My dreamland was an elusive, beautiful place where clever people who were warm and wonderful human beings talked to me. Not about things like set the table for supper . . . bring in an armload of kindling . . . blow out the coal oil lamp and go to sleep, but about ideas. Their sentences would start with gentle phrases — "I wonder if" or "What do you think?"

I loved to wonder about things. I'd cross the road from our farmyard and follow the creek through a pasture to the sawmill when the ear-splitting whine of the circular saw was silent in the evening. Its shining, jagged teeth leered harmlessly at me in the slanting rays of sunlight, while I sat high above the water wheel, watching the creek flow by, dreaming my dreams.

With every season I had a different reason for following that stream over the water wheel, through a second pasture, into the bush.

In spring, I was hunting morels. In summer, blackberries. In the fall, nuts. And come December, the Christmas tree.

My dream world, though ever changeable, remained constant over my school years. In it I would travel to people less fortunate than myself and help them. Maybe I'd be a missionary. I'd become knowledgeable about people and places. Maybe an author.

Whatever, it would be the good life.

My dream was strongest in my grade school days, when life was made up of my mother's little philosophies which turned necessity into a virtue. Waste not want not. Idle hands are the devil's tools. Do unto others as you would have them do unto you. Beauty is only skin deep. He who laughs least laughs last.

These carried over into our play. We had no television, and our radio batteries had to be saved for noon newscasts, Saturday night National Hockey League games, and maybe Sunday night Lux Theater, if reception was good.

We had no Y program or private lessons, but that didn't deter us. We learned to play publicly on the mill pond with skates strapped to our snowboots. Dad skated with us, his big blades buckled to his barn boots. He always took an old chair from the summer kitchen to help the learners among us. Often he sat on it, watching us, or just staring off to the westerly hills.

Being five years younger than my older sister, I had to try harder, until this effort became the norm for me. If she ridiculed my performance, I reminded her, "I could do better than you'cordingly," and I did.

Then the war was declared, solemnly, by King George VI over the noon newscast in that very British voice of the BBC in London, England.

In the following years of rationing — butter, meat, sugar, and gasoline — we cared not a hoot about not having things, for nobody else had them either.

With industrial supplies and consumer goods frozen, new appliances, cars, and farm machinery were unheard of. Even electrical wiring required special priority, which dad's mixed farming didn't rate.

So with no hydro, no milking machines, and farm hands leaving for war plants and the army as soon as they were old enough, my chores extended from after school until long after dark. I did my homework alone, by lamplight, long after everyone else was in bed.

Sometimes a new hired hand, too young for the army, would sit up and read the English words from my textbook, while I spelled the Latin conjugation back to him. When he found I was more interested in Latin than in him, he wearied and went to bed too.

Sometimes I'd doze before my homework was finished and wake to darkness and the coal-oily smell of the lamp burned dry. I'd rub myself warm by the kitchen wood stove, dampered for the night, and dash to bed in our unheated upstairs. After shivering the bed sheets warm, I'd lie for a few minutes watching the stars twinkling through the dormer window, dreaming and praying.

It seemed but forty blinks until someone hammered on the stovepipes, awakening me to darkness. Time to do chores again. Then breakfast, hitch a ride to town on a milk sleigh, high school, and chores again.

Yet as I think of it now, Joanna, I don't ever remember feeling pushed or knowing any of the awful urgency of running to keep up.

Nor can I remember ever being lonely then.

I had thoughts to people the quiet pockets of time. I'd lean my head against a bovine shank, listen to the warm stream of milk striking the tin pail, and think my thoughts. I had ten minutes thinking time per cow in the morning. And at night I stretched it to fifteen.

Sometimes I thought of the strong circle of dependency between our animals and us. When a cow swung her head around to look at me with a sloe-eyed, placid stare, I wondered what she thought of this human robbing her of milk.

When I asked dad about it, he laughed heartily and said I had it all wrong. The cow considered me her personal maid, come to care for her needs twice daily.

And I wondered about the endless cycle of our environment — water, earth, and air — and our dependency upon them.

Dad said a good farmer respects this trinity in time — air, water, soil — and its keeper, as the Lord is our keeper in eternity. The devil is the spoiler. "And he needs no help from us," dad used to say. Though man in his greed is too often the devil's tool.

With gasoline rationed, new cars nonexistent, and living two miles beyond everything, much of our life was made up of walking. Walking sets a good pace for day-dreaming. So my dreams grew stronger. Life had a sense of worth then.

Joanna, I feel this so strong in memory. How could I have lost it?

What I have written thus far is a simple story of a happy child. Probably a dozen others raised in that area where the Niagara Escarpment runs into Georgian Bay could have written similarly, for that's the way it was then.

It was the real era of do-it-yourself, predating today's paint by numbers, plastic kits, and dye-cut models. None of us needed an easy-bake oven. We learned to wrestle with the real thing, baking in a wood-fired oven. It wasn't play — but it was fun.

Even in our play we had none of the precut, pseudo-situations. It was for real.

Break the ice, and you got soaking wet. There was always one case of pneumonia every spring among us. How did we know the ice was no longer safe unless someone fell through?

In our *mouse trap* games it was a real enemy — little, gray vermin that ate a bushel of grain each per month from fodder bins.

When we went *kerplunk*, it wasn't little plastic marbles that fell, it was us — down the hay shoot. If we overjudged our bounce while unclogging the hay shaft, we'd overshoot the crib and land kerplunk in the bull pen.

Life was worth living then!

Joanna, there's that sentence again, with all that it implies. I must have decided, for some reason, that life is no longer worth living. But it was subconscious, because I don't know why!

But I can see that the happy child with her childhood dreams bears only the remotest relationship to the woman who stood in the water wanting to end it all.

That child longed for life and went out after it. High

school proficiency awards, the school basketball team, and contests of every kind. She was always in there trying, story and essay contests — I like . . . in twenty-five words or less. She collected contest entry forms like some girls collected pretty ribbons and fancy china.

She tried them all, and won some. First prize of sixty cents in a hobby contest with an embroidered cushion cover. Fifty cents for second prize in a map-making contest at the Bruce County Exhibition. A short story contest won her a large dictionary. First prize in a public-speaking contest took her on her first trip to the city and overnight in the King Edward Hotel, Toronto.

These were the small awards of a post depression era, but they add up to a picture of a girl with the will to win. A girl so unlike the loser that walked to the dock, or the face I meet in my mirror, that I seriously question her existence.

Maybe she is only the figment of my imagination. After all, imagination is a writer's stock in trade.

But I know she existed, Joanna, for I have a picture of her. A girl in a frumpy dress with bloomers bagging below the hem, short-cropped hair with bangs cut high over her happy smile.

Suddenly, clear as the summer day on which the picture was taken, I remembered it.

Uncle Rusty, my father's youngest brother, home from the States where he worked in a motor plant. He gave us the first candy-coated chewing gum I'd ever seen. He had a camera, the first I'd ever handled, and he used it with extravagance, taking pictures of all manner of things that pleased him and puzzled the adult relatives. A crumbling stone castle on the mountain, the mill wheel in motion spraying out splashes of sunlight. And Captain.

That Captain! He was a magnificent beast. Hitched to a buggy or cutter, he brought us through more than one flash flood and sudden snowstorm that a lesser animal couldn't have.

But Captain thought field work menial and beneath him. He so cleverly avoided it that it seemed wicked to betray the proud beast. He would pasture with the herd of milk cows, his head hung low to hide his pale mane, moving forward on his foreknees so he wouldn't stand taller than the cows closed around him.

Then when grandfather or father had given up looking for him, I'd race to the pasture and give Captain a slap on the rump. With one strong backward thrust of his shoulders he'd leap from his knees to his front hoofs, fling his mane, and whinny his thanks before prancing off down the gully, his tawny roan tail flying free in the warm summer breeze.

The following Christmas Uncle Rusty sent us copies of the pictures he'd taken. I slipped mine out of its black, holding corners and turned it over. In his rapid scrawl he'd written, "Keep swinging, kid. You'll make the big league someday."

It's been years now since I've seen Uncle Rusty Bender. The last I heard of him he'd retired from the motor plant and was exploring his ancestry in Germany, which sounded so much like I remembered him from that summer.

But what has happened to me? I haven't made the big league in anything, Joanna. More than half of my allotted three-score-years-and-ten are gone. I'll never make the big league in anything now!

Suddenly that feeling of drowning washed over me again. But with it came other memories.

After I finished high school, I went to the city to work. When the war ended, I went to college. But when I came home on holidays, the Captain I fed carrots and apples to bore no resemblance to the imaginative, courageous creature that had pitted his wits and strength against storms of rain and snow, and people, and won — most of the time.

Every morning Captain went out to pasture with the cows. Every evening he came in from pasture with them. *Captain had become a fat cow.*

And so have I!

Joanna, Joanna, I found my cow pasture. And *I am the cow.*

Every morning I get up and go to the kitchen, around the house, and to the garden, working all day as repetitious as a cow chewing her cud — twelve or sixteen hours a day — working, working, working. Come night I go and lie down. And like a stupid, placid cow, I'll do the same thing tomorrow.

Come winter, when the garden is bedded in straw and covered with snow, I'll be penned in, stabled. But I will still wake at the same time and work at the same work — food, clothes, and clean house for the family — and do the same thing the next day.

Like Captain, I've turned into a fat cow.

Joanna, I don't want to be a cow. I want to live.

I want to be a human being. I want all the Lord intended me to have as a human being.

HELP!

Chapter 7

Welcome to the human race!

And what a wonderful creature of divine workmanship a human being can be! A thinking, feeling, worshiping being, this God-planned entity, whom the angels in heaven look at in envy.

Read about it in 1 Peter 1:10-12.

The prophets found it was not to themselves, but to us, that He came in His fullness. The patriarchs, prophets, priests, and kings, even the angels, never had this enviable position — a body as the habitat of the Holy Spirit. Only in us, after Calvary, after Pentecost, did the Comforter come to *dwell*.

And you, Allison Bender Hughes, as a human being, are offered salvation, that love-paid ransom of body, soul, and spirit.

You, as a human and partaker of the redemption offered, have a responsibility to feed and nurture the *body, soul, and spirit of Allison Bender Hughes*. As well as those of her children and husband.

You too are a human being.

You too are the habitat of the Holy Spirit.

Your affectionate accomplice in survival,

Joanna

Chapter 8

I am a human being. I am not a fat cow. I know this to be a fact, Joanna.

Praise be for that!

So why do I *feel* like one?

Remember, I've had a long and close relationship with cows in my growing years, and that's exactly how I feel — like a cow!

I know I've put on some weight. I've had four children in the past sixteen years, but. . . .

Then I stepped on the bathroom scales. The needle fluttered wildly and stopped at . . . 183½ pounds!

Oh, Joanna, no wonder I feel like a fat cow. I am!

What will I do? What can I do?

I grappled with ideas to beat off the feeling of panic. I can't join Weight Watchers; they meet every week. I couldn't get away regularly with Harvey's shift work. They pay fees too, and I couldn't do that. I have no income — haven't sold a story in four years. Haven't written one, either.

Harvey gives me the household budget to manage, but with it I get the bills and his instructions: "I make it. You make it go around." There's more to make it go around all the time. The family is larger and prices are higher and higher. No matter how hard I run. . . .

No, Weight Watchers is out. And so are health clubs and diet foods.

Oh, my God! How did I ever get this way? I meant no profanity. It was a cry for help.

Joanna, I knew that my glen-plaid suit and two tailored dresses, which I wore when speaking and leading services, didn't fit me any more. But since I'm not on committees like I used to be, it didn't seem to matter. I'd never taken the time to stand on the scales, not since shortly after Andy was born. I was somewhat overweight then — but 183½ pounds — that's what I weighed *before* he was born!

Why? How?

I was never fat as a child, Joanna, or obese when a college or working girl.

What do I do about it? I just can't stop eating. I've got to keep up my strength. I've got a husband and four children, an eight-room house, a lawn, a garden, and all the responsibilities of food, clothes, and housework. Harvey's family is coming for Christmas. I've got to keep going.

At that moment I felt as if the whole 183½ pounds was pressing on my head. No, it was deeper than head pressure, it was heart — heavy-hearted.

I closed the door on the scales. And with a great sigh, I sagged into my typist chair — I think better there. It creaked under my weight. No wonder! The bulge of my folded hips spread four inches either side of the chair seat — and looked like the swollen shank of a pregnant cow!

I tasted bitterness. No, not the urge to drown myself. I want to live. I am a human being. A thinking, feeling, worshiping being! A God-planned entity, whom the angels in heaven look at in envy.

But the bitter taste was still on my tongue. The flavor of failure, of being set aside, out of the running, a reject. A person gone to pot. A beer belly without any of the false bolstering of the beer itself. Twice cheated. Christians don't drink.

So what do Christians do?

Instantly, words long set aside rose within me.

If any of you lack wisdom, let him ask of God, that giveth to all men liberally, and upbraideth not; and it shall be given him. *

I've said it so often — under pressure in college, when counseling, as church secretary.

It's been so long; I must look it up. I kept on looking and found fourteen original words translated into the one English word — wisdom. I found such phrases as:

Whom I have filled with the spirit of wisdom. And I have filled him with the spirit of God, in wisdom and in understanding and in knowledge. In the hearts of all I have put wisdom. Women whose hearts stirred them up in wisdom. **

And on and on until I'd read all 224 references by 2 A.M.

In the parallel translations I read:

If any of you is deficient in wisdom, let him ask of the giving God, [Who gives] to everyone liberally, and ungrudgingly, without reproaching or faultfinding, and it will be given him. ***

* James 1:15 KJV
** Exodus 28:3; 31:3, 6; 35:26 KJV
*** James 1:5 LB

Joanna, I actually hugged that Book to me and cried. Not the silent weeping of a lonely woman, but the crying of a child, one who had run away from home, come back braced for punishment, only to find the open arms of a caring Father.

Only until then, I wasn't aware I'd been away!

The accumulation of fear, desperation, hurt, or whatever it was that drove me down that lonely walk to the dock washed away with those tears.

As I switched off the reading light and sat for a time in the half light of a full moon-set, I felt a lightness and warmth within.

The Comforter is come. I am not alone. I felt the stirring of this thinking, feeling, worshiping, nonphysical part of me.

I am more than a stomach!

I am not a fat cow with four stomachs to be fed, so I will stop eating as if I am. I am a human being with one stomach; I am the habitat of the Holy Spirit, so I must start acting as *I am.*

Run, I would have to, for come morning the race would be on again. Harvey would arrive home from the night shift, three children would scramble for the bathroom, breakfast, lunches, and schoolbooks. The fourth child and the dog would run every-which-way as I raced to keep ahead of their needs.

By the grace of God, I could learn to run more wisely.

*I therefore so run, not as uncertainly; so fight I, not as one that beateth the air.**

Slowly another verse emerged to consciousness.

*But I keep under my body, and bring it into subjection: lest that by any means, when I have preached to others, I myself should be a castaway.***

* 1 Corinthians 9:26 KJV
** 1 Corinthians 9:27 KJV

Others I had helped; myself I could not help. A cast-away! That is exactly how I felt!

Once I had popularized a Sunday school slogan — "a Scripture learned is never forgotten." Now I had a new, awe-filled respect for the necessity of memorizing verses. I must encourage my children.

> Now every athlete who goes into training conducts himself temperately and restricts himself in all things. They do it to win a wreath that will soon wither, but we [do it to receive a crown of eternal blessedness] that cannot wither. Therefore I do not run uncertainly – without definite aim. I do not box as one beating the air and striking without an adversary.
> But [like a boxer] I buffet my body – handle it roughly, discipline it by hardships – and subdue it, for fear that after proclaiming to others the Gospel and things pertaining to it, I myself should become unfit – not stand the test and be unapproved – and rejected [as a counterfeit].*

How ugly the truth is, even when beautifully written. Running without a goal. Beating the air. How often I'd done just that, frantically waving my arms in warnings: "Don't wake your father. Quiet, quiet. Shh, your father is sleeping." They must wonder if I have a windmill among my ancestors.

Suddenly for the first time in years, I had a definite, positive aim related to me! To remove 46½ pounds of ugly fat! To discipline my body that I would no longer be a counterfeit Christian!

Finally I lay down to rest. It would be a long race that would start early. But the expectancy of again working toward a goal pounded through me like the exhilaration of a pregame warm-up.

It was no time until the alarm bell rang. As usual I rose, went to the kitchen, put the skillet on the stove, opened the refrigerator door, and remembered. Today I diet!

*1 Corinthians 9:25-27 AMPLIFIED

I went back to the bedroom and started again — this time on my knees — and read again, and again, and again:

> Like an athlete I punish my body, treating it roughly, training it to do what it should. . . . Otherwise I fear that after enlisting others for the race, I myself might be declared unfit and ordered to stand aside.*

That's exactly how I feel! Life is passing me by.

After Grace was born, I had the care of a new baby and a three-year-old. I no longer had time to write. Then when Mark was born, Harvey transferred to the night shift, and I had to drop all evening activities, prayer meeting, women's missionary work nights, and the Christian Education Committee.

After Andrew was born, church nursery facilities were limited and badly handled in our little church in the village, so I offered to help there. But Sunday became just another day of child care for me. Mothers left their young children with me to rush off and sit with their husbands in church. The nursery entrance was under the main doorway, and I heard the rumble of footsteps as everyone passed overhead.

Joanna, I stood aside in the home.

After I piled last night's collection of schoolbooks on the table by the door and laid each child's school lunch by his place at the table, I stood aside for the rush as they passed, reaching for lunches with their right hands and books with their left, calling, "Bye, mom."

I stood aside for Harvey as he rushed in from the garage to grab some of his early supper set out for him, warning us: "I'm going to be late for work, so if you don't wantta get tramped on . . . Heh! Heh! Heh! . . ." I kept Andrew and myself well out from under his steel-toed work boots.

I stood aside when grocery shopping, squeezing closer to the shelves to let others past as I calculated the

* 1 Corinthians 9:27 LB

cost per ounce of the announced bargains as compared to those cans behind or on lower shelves.

Publishers no longer sent me authors' copies of their periodicals or writers' tips for upcoming markets.

Passed by in every area of my life!

After having proclaimed to others the gospel, I myself was disqualified. I accepted the real feeling of failure due me, not with any outward tears, just the salty taste of inward tears.

Then before my praying eyes paraded faces I hadn't thought of in years. Faces of children I'd taught in Sunday school, children I'd "dwelt with" in Good News Bible clubs, day camps, park work, vacation Bible schools. Holding their remembrance prayerfully, I calculated their present ages, speculated on their possible circumstances, and prayed for each.

Something warm and wonderful crowded close.

Twenty-two minutes later, I rose, rushed to the kitchen, awake in every part of me except my stomach. Inside I was filled with a swelling sensation like joy.

When the first rush of morning passed — the children in school, Harvey in bed, Andy and Scout outside — I made myself a strong cup of hot coffee and sat down. I drank it, hot, clear, black.

I didn't know coffee tasted like that!

I've drunk gallons of it in the past years, usually tepid or cold, and never without cream and sugar.

Today I determined I would sit down and have breakfast with a book and break the awful fast of my mind. I spread out four versions of Scripture on one side of my steaming coffee and an analytical concordance on the other.

Suddenly, I looked over my shoulder, wondering what Harvey would think if he awoke and saw me sitting here reading, at nine o'clock in the morning.

Harvey hasn't much patience with reading. When people ask him if he's read my books, he shrugs and replies, "When I read, I want something that's true. Not some made-up story." But he never does.

Well, this is Bible reading. Harvey believes it to be the inspired Word of God, even though he doesn't read it himself any more. And for good measure, I reminded myself defensively, *I have a soul.* I have a right to feed my soul too!

Read I did. Everything about fat. All 41 original words translated into some form of the English word *fat,* in at least 115 references.

More than an hour later I reluctantly left my books spread out on the back half of the kitchen table in hopes of catching a minute between my trips from washer to dryer to kitchen sink to refrigerator in today's run.

The books were still there untouched when Harvey came out of the bedroom in his pajamas at 3:00 P.M. and sat at the table for his breakfast.

"What's all this about?"

While he ate four slices of bacon, two eggs, three slices of toast with butter and jam, washed down by three cups of tea, I told him all about it. How I'd discovered the reason for that midnight walk to the dock.

"My feeling of failure *was* real. I was spiritually set aside, by-passed, rejected, a castaway. I used to know the answers. Now I don't even know the questions. Harvey, I've become a *consumer only,* never producing anything. I am a counterfeit Christian!

"Harvey, even if I have to go on working eighteen hours a day doing things that will just have to be repeated tomorrow, at least I am not going to be as big a consumer. I'm going on a diet!"

"Diet? What do you want to go on a diet for?"

"Because I have a goal: to lose 46½ pounds in the next

year! And I'll get to know myself, and break some of the bad eating habits — "

"I don't see anything wrong with our eating habits. I should think you'd be grateful for the good food you get to eat. Here I work my butt off so you and the kids can have all this — " He stabbed a clenched fist at the cupboards and refrigerator-freezer. He pounded the tabletop. "With half the world going hungry, and you come up with a fool idea like that! If you want to go all spiritual over food, then act a little *thankful* for what I've worked hard to give you!"

Joanna, I tried to reason with him, explaining the Scripture link between fatness and the loss of feeling and understanding.

> *Jeshurun waxed fat* . . . covered with fatness; *then he forsook God* which *made him, and lightly esteemed the Rock of his salvation.**

I tried to explain to Harvey that that's what I had done. That suicide is the act of a person who has lost her sense of values — lightly esteeming the Rock of salvation. And how I'd heard "love paid the ransom for me" and didn't want to drown.

Harvey refused to believe it was anything but a bad dream, that I could forget if I wanted to, *if he insisted.* But I held onto my goal. "It'll work, Harvey. I'm sure it will!"

"Just don't try serving any of your dumb diet stuff to me!" He spotted two fresh rhubarb pies still steaming on the counter. "Hey, hey, hey, what'ya got there? How about a piece?"

"For breakfast? They're still hot. Rhubarb pie doesn't taste good hot."

"Says you! Put some ice cream on it. That'll cool it down."

So I set it before him, just as he ordered. He smacked my cow-sized shank. "Nobody likes to feel a skinny woman. I like you the way you are."

*Deut. 32:15 KJV

"Well, I don't. I hate myself like this. I'm a fat cow doing the same thing today that I did yesterday and will do tomorrow, like a cow chewing her cud — the same motions over and over and over again, going nowhere."

"Oh, so that's it! You're fed up with the kids and me. You've got some fool female idea of being a college glamour girl again." His words spurted out around mouthfuls of half-chewed pie. "You don't need any diet. You're a married woman. With four kids."

"I'm a thinking, feeling, worshiping being!"

"You're my wife!"

This is Harvey's ultimatum to everything. The phrase that ends all arguments. This time he punctuated it with a slam of the bedroom door as he went back to bed.

I stood by the kitchen table silently declaring, "I still have a soul. I do, I do, I do."

I said it to myself for an hour. I was still saying it when I noticed *two* empty plates on the table.

Two?

I was the only person in the house besides Harvey. Two empty plates? And two empty spaces in the pie?

I'd devoured a piece of pie, *unaware that I'd eaten it!*

Oh, Joanna, Joanna. Maybe angelic beings envy men, but *angels in heaven don't envy women the souls they're not allowed to use.*

Chapter 9

Every time I reread the last line of Allison's letter, I felt the loneliness in it all over again.

Angels in heaven don't envy women the souls they're not allowed to use.

To that she might easily have added, *I might as well be dead! It was the same silent cry. How does one answer such anguish?*

Very carefully!

So very carefully I reread all of Allison's letters, as an author does the earlier written chapters of a book to catch the mainstream of the story problem before moving ahead into a new phase of the story. Otherwise one can follow a tributary action which drains off interest rather than building up suspense to the climax.

Only what I had here was the reverse. For I, Joanna, am not the author who is on the inside of the story looking out. I am really the reader on the outside looking in and, as such, view each new situation presented with the plumb line of real-life experience in a reader's attempt to recognize the true source of the story problem and its true solution.

How does one, off in a field of tribuatries? Of course. Follow upstream to the source.

Oh. Oh. My husband warned me about nonprofessionals. Those helpful humans who in the name of love meddle in other peoples problems are the most lethal of all. Someday you'll open a can of worms. . . .

A soul I'm not allowed to use. . . . Says who?

With Allison's inquiring mind she must know the who behind her feelings by now, when a simple phrase, "Says who?" added to her cry could clue me in from this distance.

As a writer, Allison's characterizations had been one-dimensional and her problems shallow, but she was no amateur with words. She knew how to develop ideas to a logical conclusion. So she must have known, subconsciously at least, for some time now that her stories of too-nice situations, too-good people in a too-nonphysical world of Christians was an overcompensation for the lack of such in her real-life "Christian" situation.

In her letters to me she had already touched on such tributary problems as severe headaches, obesity, sleeplessness, loneliness, hunger for beauty, loss of identity, loss of self-worth – all symptoms of the suicide syndrome. So by now, a conscious awareness of the source could have surfaced. For anything less than honesty at this point would only be another ivory-tower tactic pulling her into more tributary problems.

The lid was off! Allison's own words about her iron-kettle headaches which lifted when she read the Scriptures or books on the humanities.

So what does one say? Your husband is your problem – but he's not your enemy. Your enemy is Satan. What help is that? She still has to live with her husband.

Equal doesn't stay equal. No, I've said that before. To

say it a second time would sound too much like I told you
so.

What all have I said? Too much, probably.

*But I cannot sit, hands in pockets, when she writes her
heart out! I am a writer. I will write to her with plain
woman-to-woman understanding.*

Even her husband shouldn't object to that!

Evanston, Illinois
Wednesday, November 21

Dear Allison,

You make my mouth water with that rhubarb pie!
Why don't you write a cookbook?

But, Allison, don't make a moral judgment on yourself
over one piece of rhubarb pie. The older I get, the more
aware I am that right and wrong are relative. Only God is
absolute!

*Every athlete who goes into training conducts himself
temperately and restricts himself in all things.**

Let that go for guilt too. It is unlikely that you are
absolutely wrong, as one is rarely absolute right, so don't
condemn yourself as if you were.

A goal of 46½ pounds is no sprint, but rather a long-
distance run, so keep your eyes on the goal and keep going.
Every runner hits bad ground sooner or later. It's a normal
hazard of racing. I'm sorry you bit the dust so soon out of
the ivory tower. Or should I say, hit the rhubarb pie?

Use an old Sunday school technique — short-term
prizes for accomplishments, adding up to an annual pin or
award. You know the bars and stars routine? In your situation make it a new blouse at nine pounds, a special dessert
at sixteen. At twenty-three a new skirt. At twenty-six make
a simple dress of a color you've never worn before, but
have had a secret yen to. Buy a pattern for a complete outfit
— the smartest style you can find. One you can see yourself

* 1 Corinthians 9:25 AMPLIFIED

wearing to speak at a convention of a thousand writers. Tape a picture of it on the refrigerator door.

When shopping, keep your eyes open for material for that suit, but make it good quality. Missionaries have a saying borrowed from some shrewd Scotsman — "We can't afford to buy cheap."

Pick up color-tones in scarves, pins, accessories as you can afford them.

Have you had that meal of cauliflower yet? It's your favorite vegetable, remember? And low in calories too. As are mushrooms, asparagus, and broccoli, which most cauliflower fans like also.

If Harvey won't eat cauliflower, give him fresh-frozen corn from the freezer. I've never met a man yet who didn't like that, hot and buttered.

Don't be disturbed if he sees separate vegetable dishes as the thin edge of the wedge to separate beds. Some men are so easily threatened that they see all individuality in women as unnecessary — even wrong. They don't really see a woman as an individual being, but rather, an extension of themselves. Thus the "you are my wife," implying, "therefore, you must think like me. We are one flesh. The Bible says so. And what God hath joined together, let no man put asunder."

So that takes care of me for encouraging you to separate vegetable dishes.

Sounds silly, I know, yet it is serious. Sure, I know the soul won't die for want of cauliflower. But it will for want of the decision to live as a thinking, feeling, worshiping being, according to the Scripture.

It is written, and so often quoted (by men):
They shall be one flesh.

Yes, but separate souls. There is no exchange for a soul.** Not even the marriage certificate — the document

* Genesis 2:24
** Matthew 16:25

that makes so many things right in so many instances, such as lust, anger, unrestrained passion, the laborer without hire, and so on. Even this does not dare decree that your soul is not your own.

Jesus held an attitude regarding the personal being of each soul, including women, that was distinctly different than many in the church have held, including interpretation of Paul's writings taught even today.

It took 1200 years and a man like Thomas Aquinas to write without qualms about *woman's place*. He seems to me to have started with Paul's teachings and then reverted to Greek philosophy, predating the church and Christianity, leaning heavily on Aristotle, a student of Plato, for his fortification against women as thinking, feeling, worshiping beings.

> *The image of God is found in every man, but this does not apply to woman, since she was made in the image of man, not God.*

> *Should women have been made in the first production of things?*

> *No, since the female is a misbegotten male, and nothing misbegotten should have been in the first production of things.*

> *Since subjection and limitation are the result of sin, therefore it was said of woman: Thou shalt be under man's power. It was necessary that woman be made, but as a helper to man. More specifically, as helper in the work of generation, for other work can be done more efficiently by man.*

> *Further, woman is naturally subject to man because in man, the discernment of reason predominates.*

> *Should woman have been made from man? She should not have been!*

> *Sex belongs to man and animals, and in other animals the female was not made from the male. She should have, since this gave the first man a certain dignity.*

> The image of God is found in every man, yes. But this does
> not apply to woman, since she was made in the image of
> man, not God.

In Christianity, the further away one wanders from the
source, in this case Jesus Christ, our Lord, the weaker the
reasoning, and thus the more need for fortification to hold
such a falsified view.

Thus, strange cultural developments varying in form
from local churches to national assemblies cover multi-
combinations of philosophies from Plato, Aristotle, and,
Aquinas onward, and are never more noticeable than to
the young missionary on her first furlough.

When doing deputation in the Midwest, I wore a
tweed traveling suit, the type that would wear well until
next furlough. Several young girls who came to view the
curio table fingered the material of my sleeve, examining
the pockets, touching the buttons before exclaiming shyly,
"It's so nice."

Then I noticed these girls wore cotton dresses of a
flowered print material, as did *all* the women in the
church. This was January on the prairies, and these
weren't poor people. All the men wore dark serge suits —
all wool and a yard wide in material. Yet a woman wearing
a tweed suit in their church was more of a curio than teak
carvings, tribal drums, and a llama skin rug.

At another church the women all wore dresses made
from similar material, in the same pattern. And they nodded their heads in unison to the pastor's exhortation
against the sin of conformity from his text in Romans 12:2.

Obviously these men didn't beat their wives or mis-
treat their children. Nor were they stingy, for their giving
to missions was phenomenal for that financial era.

Being young and unmarried at the time, I was curious
about it and questioned their pastor. He promptly told me
these women had everything — a roof over their head and
food on their table. What more could a woman need?

After a week and two weekends of meeting with them, I decided the ox and ass of Mosaic law had it better than some twentieth-century wives in the church age — the animals had had a day off duty! Where else but in pagan societies and Christian marriages is food and sex supplied on demand without argument by a woman on duty 24 hours a day, 365 days a year?

Many wives, suffering from headaches, have heard the male logic, "Why do you need a holiday? You don't go to work for your living. You're home all the time. You just live!"

Loneliness?

"Why should a woman be lonely?" reasons the male logician. "She's got the children. And a husband. And when he's away, the home."

Allison, I was too young on that furlough and too inexperienced then to either understand or accept such puzzling incidents seriously. Now that I am much older and can add, it adds up to a blanket attitude in some Christian subcultures that *individuality in women is wrong.*

Female individuality is somehow frightening to some men. It makes them uncomfortable, gives them a "not OK" feeling; therefore, they label it as wrong. And since men are the church policy-setters, it is labeled wrong by the church. But these men are also Christians, so they must have a right reason for saying individuality is wrong in women. So they say, "*You are my wife.*"

That is a true statement which no wife is going to dispute. And a neat phrase that covers many things a man would not dare say, and might even feel ashamed of saying. Such as, "You are my wife; therefore, your place is in my home with the rest of my possessions, which are covered by my house insurance against loss, damage, or any act of God."

And since the husband does not say it in so many

words, any wife who would accuse him of implying it is falsely accusing her provider, her benefactor, and is therefore a complaining, railing wife — and you know what the Scripture has to say about them!

For the most part, a man does not see his own wife as an individual. Nor does he see other women as individuals either. They are the boss's wife, the neighbor's wife, the telephone operator, the bank clerk, the supermarket cashier.

And women who don't fit into such comfortable categories, he sees as women wanting to be men, wearing the pants in the family . . . selfish . . . stubborn.

Once I heard two dedicated medical missionaries talking of a third, equally dedicated, equally skilled. "It'll be a long time before that one gets married — too independent, too selfish, a know-it-all."

The two talking were men, the third was a woman.

I haven't heard that phrase, *you are my wife*, for years. And now that I am older it sounds to me like the attention-getting call of a child who has no reasonable recourse, so uses an unreasonable one. The right to reason the validity of church clichés is not often open to women and children.

The saddest part of this is the loneliness a woman suffers thinking her situation is unique and somehow her fault. Most women don't talk about it. As you wouldn't have, had I not been hundreds of miles away and a stranger to your family as well as a writer, and thus a student of Christianity and characterization.

The idea of talking about one's husband to a Christian friend arouses negative feelings ranging from discourtesy and bad taste all the way to disloyalty and betrayal.

But where else can a Christian woman go for understanding in her need for human individuality, a need God implanted in us all? The pastors are men, the deacons are men, the Bible teachers are men, as are the majority of doctors and psychiatrists. As long as theological seminaries and divinity schools exclude women from pastoral studies, the church won't develop a full appreciation of half of humanity's spiritual problems.

The woman missionary on furlough has more freedom in the church than other women. Yet even she is given the oddest time slots — after evening services when the pastor has had all of three services at his disposal; Sunday school, where the support is small change or a prayer, too often on a monthly basis.

Once when given a meeting in the sanctuary, I was instructed *not* to stand behind the pulpit — that was reserved for ordained clergy, all men. Another chairman of a church board pointed to a spot in front of the mourners' bench, explaining that women speakers always spoke from the floor. Once I embarrassed a church secretary by publicly asking for a neck cord so I could use the public address system without standing behind the sacred desk. Microphones and sound systems seem to have had masculine connotations in church circles at that time and were therefore forbidden to women in the more chauvinistic ones.

Allison, I tripped over so many local taboos that first furlough, and since, that maybe it was just as well that my missionary career as such saw its demise before my second term was completed. For by then I was no longer surprised, but resentful of the pettiness of the pecking order propagated within some Christian assemblies.

Thank the Lord for your children. For women who have growing children with a sense of humor are the fortunate ones. They have someone to laugh with over the absurdities around them. This is so important, for laughter neutralizes the acid sting in chauvinism.

Once in a city-wide campaign I saw a youth shuffled aside in the counseling area. Maybe the counselors had a reason which I didn't know. They were busy, and some with great need went forward every night. I only knew it looked bad from where I sat in the balcony, so I started to edge toward the aisle. My son Tim put a hand on my arm — "I'll go, mom. You've got the wrong kind of plumbing."

This coming from my son startled me, until I saw the twinkle in his eyes and the fast wink with the left. We were both laughing inside, even in this most serious moment.

Male counseling male has some validity, I guess. Especially in an extended counseling situation. Yet what my sex has to do with my spiritual capacity to counsel, I don't quite comprehend. Either I have the spiritual capacity and the scriptural knowledge to help, or I don't. I should be ruled out for mental and spiritual reasons — not my plumbing.

It is funny, Allison, when you have someone to laugh with you.

Solomon said it:
*A merry heart doeth good like a medicine: but a broken spirit drieth the bones.**

Laugh, my girl, for arthritis you don't need.

Allison, the real aid to soul growth into a whole being came from Jesus of Nazareth, even before He paid that high-priced ransom.

Jesus accepted a woman's faith: Luke 13:11-13. Publicly, in the street, in a time and culture which considered women in the street and street-woman as one, He saw her and He called her to Him.

"Woman, thou art loosed from thine infirmity." He touched her. This woman, bowed together for eighteen years, was loosed by His touch!

What a record put there for uptight women of all ages — *loosed by His touch.*

A woman's faith is acceptable to the Lord Jesus Christ.

Jesus expected woman to grow in her soul: Matthew 9:20-22.

* Proverbs 17:22

A woman, whose life was wasting away from hemor-
rhaging for twelve years, touched the hem of His garment.
Jesus turned and spoke to her, publicly, in the street.
"Daughter, be of good comfort; thy faith hath made thee
whole."

Whole in her soul. The terrible draining of her
strength stopped. The shrinking of her person ceased.
Jesus comforted her. She became a completed woman.

Woman's only limitation is herself: Matthew 15:28.

Jesus tells it plainly: "O woman, great is thy faith; be it
unto thee even as thou wilt. And her daughter was made
whole from that very hour."

With her desires straight, she reached, and she received.

"Be it done for you as you desire" — the Revised
Standard Version.

Allison, I'm not going to hand you all the old cliches
— if you love enough . . . if you pray about . . . if you have
faith. Oh, they're not wrong. In fact, they're right. But they
are not enough to help when you hurt enough to say,
*Angels don't envy women the souls they're not allowed to
use.*

You need understanding of your situation as well.

Chauvinism is a masculine fortification that keeps
women in physical, repetitive, nonproductive roles. E.g.:
food, clothes, and cleaning services. Except for child-
bearing, saving the mental and spiritual careers for themselves — except where children and menial works are con-
cerned. Thus a woman with mental and spiritual abilities,
desires, and training, who fills only a physical servitude in
life, will certainly feel that angels don't envy her a soul she
is not using. And she is right!

For you to accept this limitation is a decision based on
all feeling and no faith, which is the second stage of
growth, after *all* faith and no feelings.

It seems we humans are prone to learn by overcorrecting. Remember how it was when you were learning to drive a car? First the white line loomed up under the left wheel. A pull of the steering wheel and the right wheel hit the curb. After a couple more readjustments of lesser degree, you could steer an even course in one lane, with eyes cast far enough ahead to catch possible danger in time to circumvent it.

First faith and no feeling, followed by feeling and no faith. By the time you get this letter, Allison, you will have adjusted your learner's sights between feelings and faith to run an even course.

Your husband is not likely to change his ultimatum, *You are my wife,* and all it implies. He may want you to mirror his views, remain a yes-person in the organization of the home, and fulfill all of his orders, but *he is not your enemy.* He does not want to kill your soul, warp your spiritual growth into bitterness and uselessness — *that is the work of Satan.*

What your husband doesn't anticipate is the fact that a soul kept inactive does shrink.

Regardless of the whoever and the whyever of your problem, the only one who can change is YOU. Go to it!

I like the girl you used to be — entering contests, accepting challenges, improvising, working, lacking in nothing. I caught a glimpse of her again in your Scripture research on fat and the challenge you accepted from 1 Corinthians 9:25-27 to function wholly as God created human beings — physically, mentally, and spiritually.

It says something to me, too. There is only one day to diet, and that's today.

Since you have a personal acquaintance with horses as well as cows, I can say, "Gee a little, girl." Not all faith without feelings, not all feelings without faith.

Feelings can give you a true reading of what your

needs are. And faith will help you reach a fulfillment of your real needs.

Send me a snapshot of yourself as you progress so I can rejoice with you in goals reached. Exercise your soul to win this spiritual race.

I'll be praying.

Your continued accomplice in your continued survival.

Joanna

Chapter 10

Shale Bay, Ontario
Monday, December 3

Dear Joanna,

You were right!

When I served cauliflower for dinner Sunday evening last, he actually said, "Humph. It'll be separate beds next!"

I could hardly believe my ears. How could you know?

I had to concentrate on the questions the children were asking about cauliflower so I wouldn't burst out laughing. Harvey wouldn't have seen the humor in it, even if I did explain. And he can't bear laughter he doesn't understand.

So I replied to Mark, "Yes, you are eating the flower part of the vegetable. No, it isn't a new invention. Grandpa grew them. I had cauliflower often when I was a child."

"Well, I didn't!" Harvey exploded. "And I don't intend to start now."

I set a casserole of baked corn in the center of the table

between the cauliflower dish and a platter of sausages. And I enjoyed my Sunday supper without apologies to anyone. It's the first time I've tasted cauliflower in seventeen years. Is it really that good, or was it the pleasure of individual choice that tasted so delicious?

Jeremy and Grace seemed to like their first taste of it. The two younger ones, Mark and Andrew, thought it rather dull eating compared to corn.

As we washed the dishes, all four children were comparing their views on whether we should grow some in the garden next summer. Harvey cut in, "You kids make me sick! Can't you talk about anything except that stupid cow-plop vegetable your mother thinks is so fancy?"

Suddenly I knew why I hadn't cooked cauliflower all these years. It was as if one honest expression of such a simple human feeling as "I like cauliflower" freed me to face another; for though long submerged, it now surfaced. The scene broke into my conscious mind complete like floodlight suddenly turned onto a darkened stage-set.

It was September, about six weeks after we were married. Harvey had come home late from work — blustered in, in a great rush of explanation about trying to track down the owner of a snow-blower that'd been sitting all summer in tall grass on a vacant lot.

He sat down, unfolded his newspaper to the "Miscellaneous for Sale," and after a curt "blessing" served himself and turned his attention to his paper.

With the first forkful of food, he let out an explosion, half-roar and half-cry, spitting out a mouthful of food that spattered the dinner rolls and butter dish.

I looked at him in shocked silence. Harvey had never acted like this before.

"What's this stuff you're feeding me?"

My first speechless surprise turned to stunned disbelief as his lips curled down in a double line like an inverted happy face. The base of his nose pinched back into two

white spots, his eyes shot pale blue arrows of anger —
straight at me.

"What are you trying to put over on me? That's not
potatoes!"

"No. The potatoes are here!" I lifted a china lid from a
matching vegetable bowl. "That's cauliflower. If you'd put
down your paper, you'd see — "

"Are you telling me I can't read my newspaper in my
own house? If you wouldn't hide food under lids, a man
could see what he's getting!" He heaped a double serving
of potatoes onto his plate, almost emptying the bowl, and
growled, "Cauliflower? Who'd want to eat anything called
cauliflower? *Sounds like cow-plop!*"

I was too stunned by his rudeness to answer, and too
guilty for having triggered it to ever serve cauliflower
again. I never planted it in the garden. I don't remember
noticing it on the produce counters at the supermarkets. I
must have blocked it out of my thinking — until it popped
out when I started my story files on the girl at the dock.

Now that the unstuck feelings have begun to unwind,
there seems to be no stopping them.

Last week I scraped the last of a roast turkey from its
bones, looked at the two cups of bits and pieces — the
sweetest meat is close to the bone — and exclaimed,
"Look, kids. There's enough for a good bowl of turkey
chowder for us."

Then this double-thought I've developed in researching myself came back with, "Why *us?* Why do I always
make chowder for a meal when Harvey isn't going to be
home?"

And it happened again. The memory reel started to
roll out a long-forgotten scene, beginning with dialogue
this time.

"Hmm, something smells good." It was Harvey's
voice. I lifted the lid from a two-quart china chowder bowl
to show him its contents — turkey chowder.

"You don't expect me to eat that gooey mess? How do I know what's in it?" Harvey's lips pursed into a Donald-Duck beak, and his eyes narrowed into a blue squint as he stomped to the cupboard for the peanut butter jar.

"I don't expect *you* to know what I put in it. *I'm* the cook. I've been cooking and caring for you for three months now. *Why* would you have to know what all is in it?"

While I sat straight on my chair, primly eating one of my favorite menus — turkey chowder with tossed salad and hot buttered biscuits — Harvey ate his peanut butter and onion sandwich loudly and smellily, drowning out all the pleasure I should have had in creating a renowned family recipe.

So I dropped chowder from my thinking too. Until one day mother reminded me what a nourishing and economic food it was for children old enough to begin eating from the table.

Rita, Harvey's younger sister, dropped in one day when the kids and I were having a chowder supper. Now she'll ask when she phones from the city, "Don't forget to call me next time you have that 'goodie bowl' again. Your gourmet cooking is wasted on Harvey."

But I never served it to Harvey again.

Having it became a happiness time for the children and me — as I can see now that it was for my mother and grandmother before me. Grandma served chowder with tea biscuits at her quilting bees for the United Farm Women of Ontario. And for dessert, more hot tea biscuits with a tray of homemade fruit jellies to choose from. Afterwards she'd send a two-quart jar of chowder home so John and the hired men could have a taste for supper too.

Now that I think of it, so many of the fun-times the children and I enjoy are the meals when Harvey isn't home. Like our happy-faced hamburgers: a big grin outlined in cheese on the meat pattie. Mark's favorite is the one-eyed monster: one cherry set in the pit-hollow of a preserved peach, on a milk pudding, with shredded coconut fringing the upper half for white hair.

When we just had Grace and Jeremy, I still tried to make fun a whole family affair.

One June, Grace came home with a straight-A report card. I suggested, "Let's celebrate! Let's have a picnic."

Jeremy ran to the basement for the cooler, Grace made Kool-Aid, I filled a thermos with tea and packaged the potato salad, celery, radishes, green onions, hard-boiled eggs, and added rolls and freshly baked strawberry pie.

Harvey was on midnight shift, so I couldn't foresee any reason why we couldn't go to the beach, just two sideroads up, have a swim, and an early supper. Harvey would still have time to sleep before midnight.

The children had everything ready on the stoop when their father came home from town. He got out of the car, looking as if he'd been hunting for something in a dozen junkyards and hadn't found it. He noticed the children skipping around in anticipation.

"What's all this about?"

I told him.

"What do I want to go traipsing off somewhere to eat for? I can eat right here. Why can't you ever be satisfied? You got a roof over your head and food on the table. Why do you always have to come up with some other crazy idea?"

It had seemed like such a delightful idea, Joanna. We'd been so happy preparing for our picnic. He saw our disappointment and lashed out at me.

"Look at them! You and your dumb ideas! Making me into some kind of an ogre! When you know I've got to go to work at midnight! I'll swear you think up these things to turn the kids against me!"

"That's not true. All I wanted was a little family happiness — "

"Maybe you and the kids have time for happiness, but I don't! I've got to go earn the living. I don't have time to sit on my behind at home and dream up dumb ideas. . . ."

I could feel the hurt of the children, so I tried again for their sakes. "You don't go to work till midnight. It'll only take an hour and a half. It won't cost more than a gallon of gas. Why can't we?"

A bundle of keys crashed on the gravel at my feet. "If it's that important, you take them."

Going to the beach with one teary-eyed girl and one frightened boy, a knot in my stomach, and a pain creeping up the back of my neck wasn't a family happiness time or any kind of a celebration, but if the children. . . .

But they were already lugging the cooler between them into the house. So I followed and set out our picnic foods on the kitchen table. Jeremy pretended to eat. Grace tried, but went to the washroom and threw up. Harvey made a peanut butter sandwich. I ate two servings of everything.

Joanna, Joanna, how stupid can an intelligent person get?

Very, very stupid, I can see now.

It is impossible to meet a nonphysical hunger with a physical food. But try I did.

Have I so often typed the phrase *Fun, Food, and Fellowship* across Christmas concert programs, youth rally brochures, and couples' club announcements in my working days that I accepted them as a package deal among Christians?

Whatever my reasoning, or lack of it, I kept on trying. And I kept on accepting the guilt when I failed, even put-down after put-down.

Chicken and dumplings: "Who wants *wet* biscuits!"
Spaghetti with meat sauce: "I'm not Italian!"
Swedish meatballs: "Who needs foreign food!"

"It takes a good cook to make — "

"Well, I'd settle for a not-so-good cook, so I'd know what I'm eating!"

So not to let it go to waste, and in lieu of Harvey's pleasure in it, I ate heartily before the children, and it went to waist anyway — mine!

Over the years, I have found food which Harvey eats without complaint — peanut butter, potatoes, fried onions, corn, homemade bread, cookies, cakes, biscuits, all with butter on them, as well as butter tarts and fruit pies.

I've served a hot dinner any time of the day from midafternoon to after midnight. Of course with each extra meal I made, I had a cup of tea and a bite, just to be sociable.

Now I can see it wasn't social, but neurotic. *Being what one is not to get what does not exist.*

Yet I kept on trying for years for some *people* friendship, some adult conversation, a few moments of mature companionship without *thing* concerns: The car won't start. The gyrator on the washer won't engage. The septic tank is bubbling out again.

All I got was the added calories!

Joanna, I actually spent three-quarters of my waking hours planting, weeding, picking, cleaning, preserving, freezing, cooking, baking, and serving a commodity and was completely unaware of my real attitude toward it.

That's how stupid an intelligent person can be!

Joanna, just this morning the church food committee called with their Christmas entertainment requests. Their list seemed unduly large in the light of my goal — 46½ pounds off — and my hope of becoming more than a "consumer Christian."

Suddenly I heard myself asking, "Don't Christians do anything for entertainment but eat?"

Joyce, being the kind of person who can head a church food committee without coming out of it bruised and wounded, blithely replied: "Now that you mention it, no.

The permitted pastimes of the brethren seem to be food and sex. Since sex must remain in the marital bed, behind closed doors, that just leaves food for their group get-togethers."

And the sisterhood seems to suffer from the same syndrome. Bridal or baby showers, visiting the ill or the aged, at a wedding or funeral, food is our very present help, if not the focal point.

So much for the attitude to food in the Christian sub-culture. Joanna, I had to add to that my ethnic background of excellent homemakers with their German Quaker tradition of family-grown food, prepared with skill and preserved with craftsmanship.

Also I was born into a family of big eaters, with six six-foot uncles — stalwart, tight-muscled men, all weighing over 200 pounds who never mentioned calories and had never heard of cholesterol.

They were hearty men who laughed and argued and contradicted each other about the battles of the Great War, the regiment numbers of their school chums, about what girl married what fellow and moved to where. Although of Quaker stock, they were never conscientious objectors, nor did they ever dispute important or personal issues. Each respected the personal opinion of his brother. I've heard them argue the better part of an evening about the number of Hebrews who escaped from Egypt and the exact number of persons who entered the Promised Land. But they never doubted the Presence of the cloud by day, the pillar of fire by night, and manna in the morning.

I loved these strong, gentle men as a child would love six extra sides of her father. When I married, I guess I expected to keep a table which they would be proud of. And maybe I even thought all Christian men would respond to a well-kept home and the dinner bell as they did.

When the dinner bell rang, the men in my family came.

My first bitter tears in marriage were shed when I found my husband didn't answer the meal call the same way.

I remember going to the garage — a lean-to added to a lean-to on an old stable — to call Harvey. From the inner recesses of his lean-tos, he answered, "Coming." But he didn't.

Half an hour later, panic seized me. Visions of Harvey caught under one of his precariously blocked-up motors ran through my mind as I ran for the garage.

He stood over a blackened hulk of an engine, grease up to his elbows, gasoline dripping from his hand as he examined a part between thumb and forefinger before rotating it into place. He went through the same washing, examining, replacing procedure twice more before he answered: "Can't you see I'm busy, woman?"

I had fresh homemade meat pies in the oven waiting, but I said nothing. Finally I threw myself on the bed and wept. Then I ate my share and his too, doing *justice* to the no longer steaming, attractive dishes I'd prepared for my husband. I never voiced any thought of discourtesy or unkindness. Not even admitting such to myself.

Now, after waiting ten minutes for the first call, I've learned to serve the children and eat with them.

Serving cauliflower certainly didn't add one cubit to my soul, but it did give me the courage to go to the public library and begin an intelligent campaign against fat.

I stood before the bookshelves and stared with unbelieving eyes. Joanna, the whole English-speaking world must be overweight! There are books advocating everything — low-calorie diets, high-protein diets, low-carbohydrate diets, high-fat diets, books entitled *Count Your Calories* and *Calories Don't Count*, weight-loss plans that stress exercise alongside those that recommend little exercise. Other books offer convincing solutions with drugs, surgery, health clubs, diet groups, overeaters anonymous, and behavior therapy sessions. Even with all of this help right before my eyes, I still didn't know where to start.

Suddenly the Scripture solution — fast and pray — seemed beautifully simple.

Then I found there were books and rules for that too!

Fasting is a voluntary abstinence from eating, undertaken with a purpose in mind — to cleanse the body and calm the soul. That I liked. Exactly what I needed. And I was sure that fasting in my situation would include prayer — much, much prayer.

As soon as I refrigerated the frozen foods at home, I typed some of the diet data I'd garnered onto 4x8 cards where I could refer to it quickly.

Obesity is a mental state, a disease brought on by boredom and disappointment. – Cyril Connolly

My soul is dark and stormy riot, directly traceable to diet. – Gerald Johnson

I typed a new subheading in my files, now largely unused since speaking calls dropped off after the sales from my last book dwindled, and church-school teaching was curtailed by full weekend responsibility for four children, as well as having a working man's meals to cook on Sunday.

I ran my fingers over the file tabs now, as a pianist would handle neglected piano keys — longingly, with out-of-practice fingers. Thinking as I did so, *After I lay aside this 46½ pounds of extra flab, I'll have all the energy expended from packing it around on my daily run. Then I can pick up some of the mental and spiritual work dropped over the past few years of increasing responsibility in the home.*

Something to look forward to! That's what my "survival" reading advocates. And suddenly I did look forward with joy to writing, studying, teaching a Bible study group again!

Joanna, as you pointed out, my enemy is Satan, not my

husband, so I saw no reason to discuss my battleplans, but I still had to face Harvey, openly and honestly. For if I've learned anything thus far, it is the fact that there is no way to win a spiritual battle except by openness and honesty.

So I faced the first supper hour of my fast, mentally braced for the first blast!

Harvey said grace, ending with "bless this food to our use" and dropping the phrase "and us to Thy service," as daughter Grace so regularly points out to me privately.

The telephone rang. It was for Harvey. The children finished their first course, and I was removing their plates before he returned to the table. I served dessert and a second helping to Harvey at the same time. As soon as I poured tea and sat down, Harvey asked for his dessert and more tea.

I drank my tea slowly while Harvey had a second helping of dessert and more tea behind the Want Ads section of the local paper.

The kids discussed the skating rink and the pumping system they used to flood the lake surface smooth after it froze.

Nobody said a word about the food.

Nobody even noticed I hadn't eaten anything!

But two days later while doing supper dishes, Grace whispered to me, "Is it tough going, mom?"

I glanced from her secretive grin to Jeremy's smile, which Grace calls his I'm-not-as-dumb-as-I-look expression, and admitted that I'd been uptight about the first supper. But now it's wonderful. I feel cut loose from fatigue, too light for gravity pull.

I fasted eight days before Harvey noticed I wasn't eating.

It was Mark, my newsmonger, who let the cat out of the bag, with, "Hey, mom, don't you like apple pie any more?"

"Not today," I said, knowing it was the calories not

the taste of it that I had such an aversion to now.

Harvey glowered from the kids to me, from my empty plate to my half-full tomato juice glass, as if expecting it to answer if nobody else would.

I hesitated, knowing I'd have to tell all. Braced for the blast, I blurted out, "I fasted three days on clear liquid. Then these past five days I've had a glass of orange juice for breakfast, apple juice for lunch, and tomato juice for supper."

I rushed on to explain how after the first twenty-four hours my stomach seemed to go to sleep. After three days I felt exhilarated, mentally alert, and freed. My head didn't pound. My joints no longer ached. Fasting from eating is a spiritual experience —

"You can cut it out right now!" Harvey rasped out his words between whitened lips. "I can't afford to have you in the hospital. You get sick and I'll not stay home with the kids. It'll be up to Grace."

Surprised by his barely controlled anger, I blinked back the sting of tears. I couldn't look at him. I couldn't cry before the children and frighten them. I reached out for something on which to focus my own frightened feelings — a piece of apple pie.

No! No! I shoved the pie away from me, as if caught with a lethal weapon. Then I faced Harvey, telling myself in those seconds of desperate silence — Harvey is not my enemy.

"Grace is sixteen. She leaves for the school bus at 8:00 A.M. and doesn't get home until 5:00 P.M. and has a good deal of homework. How could you expect — " I bit my tongue to stop the barrage of words going nowhere. *Harvey is not my enemy.* It made no sense for me to attack his viewpoint, senseless and selfish as it seemed to me, even irrational.

Instead I silently reviewed my survival reading to myself:

Their heart is as fat as grease (Ps. 119:70).

A sound body is a product of a sound mind. – George Bernard Shaw

Hunger, the originator of thoughts. – Elbert Hubbard

After Harvey went to the garage where he can enjoy his angry silences without any family interruptions, Grace handed me some nutrition sheets given her in physical education class.

"Hang in there, mom. I'm with you."

That night I dreamed a dream.

Here Allison's typed letter ended abruptly, with an added handwritten scrawl across the bottom.

I've got to run, Joanna.
The battle is the Lord's.
Will dispatch more from the war zone shortly.

Allison

Chapter 11

Shale Bay, Ontario
Wednesday, December 5

Dear Joanna,

I dreamed a dream last night.

I've dreamed it before, but not for a long time. Not for years!

It's probably silly of me to be so pleased that I have dreamed it again — but I am. I can't explain it, Joanna, except that it is like having a happy memory happen all over again. And so strangely reassuring that I want to tell you about it right away.

I dreamed that I was at the top of Devil's Elbow ski run, about to enter a cross-country race.

I've skied on waxed hickory as well as the oak barrel staves of childhood, but only for the feel of winter sunshine on my face, the downhill wind in my hair, and the dual sense of exhaustion and exhilaration. Never in competition. Even in my college years I had no expertise whatsoever for ski racing.

Yet in my dream, there I was, lined up with business people and professionals in the racer's numbered vest. Fleetingly, in the excitement of the prerace warm-up, I wondered what I was doing among those in their sleek windbreakers, poured-into stretch slacks, sunglasses, leather gloves, ringed poles, and steel-edged, waxed hickory with gleaming safety-release bindings.

In contrast, I wore my old melton duffle coat with its tied-under-the-chin parka, home-knit mittens and muffler, and snowboots — the kind we wore to walk the unplowed roads to school in winter. And instead of skis, *I had a little red wagon!*

That's right, Joanna. A child's play wagon with small disklike wheels and a red metal box just big enough for my snowboots to fit in, side by side.

There I stood in the racing line-up of the commercially outfitted contestants, unashamed and unafraid.

In my dreaming, I remember letting my mind run over the rules posted on the ski chalet walls and deciding that for all of its hoity-toity meaning, the actual words did not disqualify me and my little red wagon, as long as I did not disqualify myself during the race itself.

It was a gorgeous sun-bright day, the kind that brings photographers and girls in bikinis to the snow-covered hills.

The PA paged Number Four to the starting position.

I poised. The gun went off. I was away.

What a beautiful, breath-taking ride through sun-sparkling snow. I drifted . . . I floated . . . I sailed.

At first others passed me, maneuvering ahead of me with flare and finesse. Others hooted in derision at my get-up and gear. But my little red wagon and I rolled along at a steady pace, up and down, around and down, down, down.

In my dream I seemed to ski for days through glorious sunlight, schussing over moguls, crossing powdery plateaus, speeding downward to sail upward again, then down, down, down.

I heard shouts from the spectators. The last ascent blocked the natural slalom to the finish line.

Roll, little wheels, roll — I willed my little wagon up and up. Momentarily I hung suspended on the crest. For an eon of anxiety I willed my red-disked wheels to roll forward to the finish line, not backward out of sight into the valley behind.

Poised in full view of the waving, cheering crowd, I prayed urgently in my heart of hearts — "Oh, Lord, forward, Lord. Help me. Forward. Hold me up, Lord. Don't let me disqualify myself *now*, Lord."

Suddenly the backward pull of gravity lifted, and I rolled forward. I felt the wagon wheels respond, rolling faster and faster as the fairy castle chalet loomed into real life before me.

Wild applause burst from the crowd as my wagon shot past a skier sprawled on the muddied south slope of the last downward stretch.

My rubber-rimmed wheels skimmed over the grass-streaked run where other skiers with their professionally designed equipment pitched down or spun out.

The cheering crowd parted to let me roll safely to a halt — across the finish line.

I made it! I made it!

I awoke with the sound of spectator cheers ringing in my ears, and my own voice exclaiming, "Me and my little red wagon, we made it!"

Oh, Joanna. It's been so long since I dreamed that dream. And it felt so good to dream it again. Like the reestablishing of a slender subliminal link to that girl who used to be — the girl who kept on trying and won some — a winner.

It's been so long since I dreamed anything but loser dreams of missing boats, or losing train tickets, or standing at the top of a flight of stairs going nowhere. It's been so long. . . .

So long, that I don't remember when — but I do.

Slowly it rose to mind. It was spring. I was sitting in the lounge chair enjoying the afternoon sun. I was pregnant with Jeremy. Grace was playing in a sandbox, making our village of Shale Bay with a plastic shovel and a great deal of imagination.

I was reading the galleys of a book, trying to decide whether to start another novel now, with summer coming on, or wait until fall. I felt heavy and tired and fell asleep in the sun.

What I thought were the cheers of the crowd milling around at the finish line of my dream turned out to be Grace screaming at the dog for digging up her village so he could bury a bone in it.

Joanna, I never did decide to start that book. But I didn't decide not to either. I just never did it — either before or after Jeremy was born. That's nearly fourteen years ago now.

That's how long it had been since I'd dreamed that dream.

Before that, I had dreamed it often — my little-red-wagon dream.

And now I've dreamed it again.

Joanna, please don't tell me I'm foolish for enjoying the sense of well-being it brings. Somehow it bridges that terrible no man's land between the girl I used to be and the overweight, overworked bundle of frustrations and failures who walked to the dock. That dream reaches across a frozen forest of unadmitted feelings to link me with me as a living, breathing believer.

My dream seems to say, "I'll make it to the finish line." I've got to, for the sake of my children!

When I lay in that nether land of dreams, remembering the last time I dreamed it, I felt a great unction to pray for my children — for their spiritual birth and growth. And I vowed more spiritual direction for them as opportunity arose.

I who had once led many children to an understanding of salvation in Jesus Christ, including my own Grace and Jeremy, had done no more for my two younger children than hear perfunctory prayers in the fatigue-deadened hour at the end of the day, putting what should be a spiritual experience on a par with endless parental orders — brush your teeth . . . wash your face . . . say your prayers . . . go to bed.

In my rush to cater to shifting work hours and increased family care and still maintain uncomplaining Christian graciousness, I'd died to everything except the urgencies of food, clothes, and cleanliness for the family.

Then I walked to the dock.

Oh, Joanna, Joanna. All of those idealistic efforts of mine to live by faith and not feelings! And all the time the subconscious was feeling. And since the subconscious is honest, it keeps tossing these honestly felt remembrances of real feelings back into my conscious mind to jolt me alive.

In being dead to feeling, I became dead in faith too!

The morning I dreamed that little-red-wagon dream, I woke and wept for joy. I was amazed all over again at the great tolerance in the love of God that had called me back that night at the dock. I was aware anew of the love-paid ransom for me.

A sense of second chance followed me through the day. And a great hunger to read the Word developed. Not just the chapter-a-day-to-keep-the-devil-away, but reading it as a thinking, feeling, believing person.

These letters to you, Joanna, are becoming *The Diary of a Hungry Housewife*. The more I discover about this being that is me, the more I know I ate to fill the wrong hunger.

Now that I am nourishing the nonphysical part of me again, my food habits are changing too. Oh, I still bake, cook, roast, and broil and spend a good part of my waking hours in the preparation of meals at all hours. But I never eat unless I am sitting down with a plate, knife, fork, and spoon set before me. I eat only when there is enough stability around me that I am aware of what I am eating. I restrict my intake to 1200 calories a day, with Sunday a free day and Monday a fast. This seems to work out a balance of eating and not eating that keeps me physically and spiritually able to cope and still lose weight.

The children think it funny when I cut myself a piece of pastry at the supper table and set it aside, saying, "I'll save that for Sunday." I store it in Tupperware when I clear the table. But next morning, because it is there and ready to go and doesn't really look all that appetizing now that the aroma of its baking is no longer in the air, I stick it in one of the kids' lunches.

In the morning, I have hot, black coffee when the children eat their breakfast. After they have their books and lunches sorted out, the right clothes on the right child, and have left for the school bus, I have my breakfast: a boiled egg and a piece of toasted cracked wheat bread.

At lunch I use whatever is around, low-caloried and bright in color. I halve it and eat it when real gut hunger strikes.

Fasting one day a week checks the natural urge to obesity and cuts off the habit of chew, chew, chewing just for the fun of chewing.

At supper, I eat some of whatever I've cooked for the whole family. The size of my serving is determined by the number of calories already consumed that day.

I find a real enjoyment in small portions served very

hot, for I've eaten so much cooled-off, leftover food that the thought of it sickens me.

If Harvey doesn't come and his food isn't usable for a reheated meal, the dog gets it — not me! Scout is getting fat. Jeremy and Mark are making a harness set so they can hitch him to a sleigh to pull Jeremy's newspapers around his three-mile daily route.

Because I eat less, I have more time to talk with the children — and to listen. Listening is a fulfilling thing, I'm finding out.

Everyone brings his frustrations home. As Jeremy says, "Where else can a kid go?" Sometimes I set both my knife and fork down to listen to a tale of Andrew's afternoon play, or a detailed account of Mark's school sporting events. Since I no longer see my children as one problematic unit, I enjoy them as individuals. One at a time, their problems can be cared for with much less tension in the normal rush periods.

When fasting, I learned to look at my children when listening to them. I am discovering other ways besides a constant barrage of parental negatives to maintain some order at mealtimes. A hand laid gently on his shoulder will get the attention of my see-all, tell-all Mark, without adding to the noise level.

Once when Andrew's loud, nonlyrical singing over his favorite spaghetti-and-meatball dinner seemed about to go on forever, I put a hand under his chin to ease that jabbering jaw closed. He glanced up at me, startled, then grinned and grabbed my hand and kissed it.

"Mom, you're gooder than spaghetti and meatballs." And that's an honorable compliment from Andrew.

So many of my old, repetitious orders are no longer needed now that the children know they will be given the courtesy of a hearing, eyeball-to-eyeball. And if not right now, just as soon as possible.

And why shouldn't they? My children have souls too!

Harvey's favorite adage, "Children should be seen and not heard," is still the law and is enforced when he is in the house. But as soon as supper is over, he goes to the garage or off on the trail of a "good deal" or somewhere, and the children can talk freely. I no longer try for one more load of washing or another batch of baking at that time of day. So they wear each pair of jeans a day longer and eat a few less pastry calories, and we are all the better for it.

Joanna, I am afraid that in the past few years I've passed on to my children the parent-to-child forms of the put-downs I accepted as limitations in my life. "You can't do that. You can't go there. You can't. Women don't. Christians shouldn't." To the children they came out as "You're too young," or "Act your age."

Joanna, my children have souls too. Souls to use as thinking, feeling, worshiping beings! Souls separate from their siblings, separate from their parents!

What a new, exciting life-interest I have. And it is not contrary to any of the ultimatums issued by Harvey's understanding of the church-sanctioned marriage relationship for wife, woman, mother, Christian. But it is the positive application of them all! To see my children grow into thinking, feeling, worshiping beings!

Life can still be exciting for me. How wonderful!

Best wishes for the coming Christmas season.

Sincerest Christian love,

Allison

Chapter 12

Evanston, Illinois
Monday, January 14

Dear Allison,

New Year's greetings to you all!

Your letter came midway through my winter bout of arthritis. This old body of mine is rebelling against the cold winds off Lake Michigan, but the word from you was like a chinook to my soul.

No, not a chinook as much as a stirring in the mulberry trees reminding me of the Lord's word to David:

> When thou hearest the sound of a going in the tops of the mulberry trees, that then thou shalt bestir thyself: for then shall the Lord go out before thee.*

And it has something to do with a phone call we received from Steve on Christmas Day that went something like this:

*

* 2 Samuel 5:24

Mom, why don't you put the buzz on dad to take that sabbatical he talks about? He could do with a change, and Cochabamba is a great place to winter.

Actually, what I am saying is, "Come over and help us." Jim and Jamie and some of their peers need a teacher. Dad's overqualified, I realize, but the powers-that-be could be persuaded to overlook that, providing he doesn't expect a salary commensurate with his qualifications.

Our kids coming up for university entrance in a couple of years have subject gaps dad could plug while enjoying a culture change – a rest missionary-style.

Mom, the Andes air is great for whatever ails you. Bring your camera, recording equipment, and come on up and write from my world for a while. How about it?

Allison, see how this being a thinking, feeling, worshiping being goes on and on — alive forevermore!

We are considering Steve's suggestion. Tom is applying for a sabbatical, and we'll take it from there, one step at a time.

Allison, I am just thrilled with the way you are turning negative put-downs into positive, believing action toward your children.

But beware! Worshiping children aren't the sweet, little angelic beings who sit in church Sunday mornings, white-gloved hands folded in picture-book style of a "child at worship"! Nor are thinking children the ones who never embarrass mother. Nor do they have much respect for anything except honesty and truth — as they see it!

A thinking, feeling child can never be counted on to be complaisant, and is too honest to be kind.

No. That's not quite true — it only feels that way to mother.

Honesty is the greatest kindness there is.

If you are tending home for four growing souls, brace yourself. Things will never be lonely for you again. Or calm either! Delightful — maybe. Wonderful — yes. Even joyful. But calm — only rarely, and then with the eerie quality of the calm before a storm.

Thinking, feeling, worshiping children make waves. That's how they become good swimmers in rough waters.

As you have learned to run in your discipline to diet, so learn to swim spiritually with these siblings in the home. Not uncertainly, without definite aim, but with the goal of proclaiming the gospel as one who can stand the test.

Strong swimmers are not obese! Or not for long anyway!

Lovingly,

Joanna

.

Chapter 13

Dear Joanna,

How can you be so right? So often?

Waves they make! Enough to make a mother seasick!

Last night I had no food on my plate. The fact being, I had already eaten my full calorie count by 4:00 P.M. And I've hung in there too long now to cheat myself and eat extra. You just can't fight figures and win. Once eaten, calories add up to overweight, whether I add them or not!

So there I sat with a cup of steaming clear tea in the center of my bare dinner plate. Harvey was in one of his moods, "Don't bother me, woman, can't you see I'm busy?" And I was just as glad. That way he wouldn't know I was skipping a meal, and I wouldn't have to listen to him reading his riot act against women who diet: "Women don't know when they're well off. Women can't face reality. Women gotta be pretty little girls all their lives."

But the kids noticed my empty plate. Grace looked puzzled, and when I didn't offer any explanation, she shrugged and ate her meat pie with healthy enjoyment, as did the boys.

Suddenly she asked, "Was Aunt Gladys here today, mom?"

I had my teacup to my mouth. Instinctively I swallowed a throat-scalding sip to keep from spewing it out with the laughter that burst inside me. "Whatever made you ask that?"

"Last week, at the intercollegiate basketball tournament, Aunt Rita asked about your dieting. She said Aunt Gladys was huffing and puffing to hear about it. She figured when Gladys got up a big enough head of steam, she'd give you a blast."

I nodded. "I ate one butter tart during her lecture on my inability to accept middle age gracefully — meaning the middle-age spread. That's what she calls obesity if over forty. Under forty, obesity is plumpness.

"And I ate a second butter tart when she mounted her soapbox on how to raise boys."

"Which one of us was it today?" Jeremy asked.

Joanna, kids have got to be natural-born writers — they won't waste words.

"Oh, she saw the wooden frame you built for practicing shots on goal with Mark."

"So what's wrong with playing hockey?" Mark demanded.

Joanna, thinking kids, yes — but do they have to be that swift? Somehow I managed to answer with a straight face.

"The dressing-room talk. A very bad influence on boys. She wouldn't let Randy or Danny play on any hockey team. . . ."

"No self-respecting hockey team would have those fairies!" Mark declared.

Grace challenged him. "Just because they play the piano better than they do hockey, it doesn't mean they are fairies."

"Does so. They are leprechauns in the St. Patrick's Day play." Mark added with a grin, "They are the only two kids in the school who play flute to suit Mrs. Barber."

Jeremy looked puzzled. "Mom, the dressing-room talk in the arena is no different than the washroom talk at school. You don't keep a kid away from either school or the washroom for that reason." He snorted. "Typical Aunt Gladys logic!"

You are so very right, Joanna! Thinking children are not comforting to the mother-ego. I'd eaten two butter tarts and worried my way through a thousand words of silent dialogue with only the *feeling* that her reasoning wasn't valid. While Jeremy pegged it in two sentences.

Grace gave us a full, mimed report of Aunt Rita's account of Aunt Gladys on the subject of my diet, and it lost nothing in the retelling.

Rita is Harvey's younger sister, a physical education teacher and coach of one of Georgian Bay's regional basketball teams.

Just then Harvey burst through the door. He never just walks through a doorway. "Tell me so I can laugh too," he demanded.

"Aunt Gladys was here this afternoon," I started to explain.

"So what's so funny about my sister?"

"Nothing," I hurried to assure him. Gladys was born without a sense of humor.

"But Aunt Rita," Grace said. "She's funny-funny."

"Humph. The laugh will be on the other side of Rita's face if she doesn't watch out. She'll be an old maid all her life! Exercising her body in public — a disgusting way for a woman to earn her living. No Christian man in his right mind would marry her now. Her and that big, flashy car!"

"Wouldn't guys date her just to ride in her Vette? Boy, that thing purrs!" Jeremy said.

Harvey dumped his meat pie upside down on his dinner plate and chopped it open to cool. "Rita makes me sick. Women who aren't content the way God made them — trying to be like men!"

Joanna, I was about to say, "Oh, Harvey, live and let live. She's earning her own living, paying her own bills," when I realized that could be exactly what rankled him about Rita.

Rita doesn't fit into the pigeonholes the church, or chauvinism, or whatever, have carved in Harvey's brain for women. She is nobody's wife. And nobody's mother. She rejects the woman put-downs Harvey comes out with — and put-downs from anywhere else too. Having repaid student loans for her own education, she now supports herself in the style of her own choosing, which includes a white Corvette.

This makes Harvey — and now that I think of it, Gladys, too — uncomfortable.

Joanna, Joanna, isn't it high time we accepted people as people, whether it be child or adult, male or female, adolescent or senior citizen? I've been thinking a lot lately about our Lord's criterion for judgment — "By their fruits ye shall know them."*

Rita is a good teacher, energetic and independent, and active in interchurch efforts.

Oh, oh! I can see that "separate vegetable dishes is the thin edge of the wedge," as Harvey said, for the honesty used to discipline my eating habits is beginning to crop up in other places too. How can I support Harvey's criticism of his younger sister when in truth Rita is an honest, interesting person?

But saying so proved to be an affront to Harvey.

"Since when have you thought Rita so great? Next

* Matthew 7:20 KJV

you'll be bellyaching for holidays in Mexico! And muscle cars!" His face darkened as his mouth bowed at the ends, drawing whitish lines on either side of his pinched-in nostrils. "Don't think you're going to get them out of me! You sit at home here while I'm out sweating, earning the living for six. You think I'm some kinda dummox that don't know what you're up to? Typing like crazy when you think I'm sleeping. Pretending you're sleeping when I come home from work thinking you'll act like a woman. I may not be educated like Rita, but I'm not so dumb I don't know you're scheming up some get-rich-quick book. I'm not so dumb I don't know your typewriter's warmer than you are when I come in off the night shift. I should start taking it to bed with me!"

He stopped midway with a mouthful of food and glowered from Grace to Jeremy. "Whadaya look so dumbfounded for? Hasn't your mother taught you nothing about *real life?*"

The children turned their undivided attention to their food. I got up to serve dishes of steaming pudding with hot carmel sauce — formerly stale Christmas cake.

I remained silent, but Harvey wouldn't leave well enough alone.

"Where's all the tee-heeing gone? You're all having a good old chitty-chatty till I come. How come all I get to look at are glum faces a mile long?"

He poked a spoon into Mark's ribs. "Cat got your tongue, kid?"

I drew in a full breath, shaping the silent words inside me — Oh, Mark, don't. Don't pit yourself against your father!

Mark answered stoically. "No. I was using my tongue to eat."

Child, child. I tried to warm him without words. Your father is not one of your school chums. He's not just another player. He's the referee too. He calls the shots.

Mark, Mark, with him you can never win.

Harvey's words hissed through clenched jaws. "You got some big-headed idea your father don't act fancy enough to suit you?"

Mark looked squarely at his father, set his spoon down, and asked, "What do you want to talk about, sir?"

For one awful minute Harvey glared at his child. The rest of us around the table waited, barely breathing.

Suddenly Harvey sputtered something inaudible and ducked behind the newspaper. He shoved his pudding dish out to me for more sauce. Once he shouted in Mark's direction, "Don't just sit there like a dummy. Either say something or get on with your supper." When he'd finished eating noisily behind his paper, he slammed out in the general direction of the garage.

Everyone let out an audible sigh.

Grace shuddered. "He's so rude! Oh, mother, why did you marry such a mean-mouthed man?" There was no criticism in her voice, just the adolescent pain of disillusionment.

"He wasn't that way when I married him." If Harvey had heard my answer, I knew he'd add, "So it's easy to see who made me that way."

Mark refused to pick up any of the hurt Grace felt. "When I was a kid and stuffed myself, he'd yell at me, 'Stop pigging yourself, kid.' I wonder what he calls it when a grownup does it?"

"Don't ask!" Jeremy warned. "I did once, and he chewed me out but good! 'Don't be such a smart-mouthed kid, and eat up. I work hard all day . . . I'm hungry . . . I pay for this . . . If you don't like the way I eat, leave the table!'"

"And you did," Grace finished for him.

Joanna, my fourteen-year-old son looked at me with adult eyes, reflecting the same query Grace had voiced. I knew he was remembering that I'd smuggled a double peanut butter sandwich up to his room.

What Jeremy can't remember is that I tried all that evening to make Harvey understand how the children felt. How I felt.

"Harvey, I know it takes a certain amount of generosity to be polite, and sometimes a great deal of effort, usually when one can least spare it. Yet if we hope to develop in our children such virtues as courtesy for others, respect for parents, and reverence for God, then we must exercise them ourselves. A Christian home can't have a double standard of behavior — one for parents, another for children."

Instead of his usual brush-off, "Don't be so stupid, woman," Harvey surprised me with a new one: "If you're so smart, why aren't you rich?"

I'd received a story rejection slip that day, so I resorted to unhappy discouraged silence. I had no answer, but after an hour or so, I added one more plea: "Won't you try when they have friends around?"

"Aw, kids are always complaining about something."

But ours aren't, Joanna. They accept his arbitrary parent control as doggedly as I do, silently hoping and praying for some caring, some sharing, some understanding that never comes.

"You and the kids make me sick. Complaining, complaining, complaining. You don't know when you're well-off. You got nothing better to blubber about than that? You don't go hungry. Why must you always be asking for more, more, more?" He stormed off to the bathroom.

I remember looking around the living room that night as if reaching for some comfort in the walls I'd painted white that summer, and the ceiling I'd stucco-plastered in a swirly pattern, and the stone fireplace I'd scrubbed until the quartz rock glittered by firelight. The embers glowed red, and I thought, I must empty the ashes in the morning when the grate is cold.

I no longer resented doing jobs like the ashes, the

garbage, the storm windows, and the yard work, but I still hated having Harvey pull that tight frown which came just before his judgmental reminder — "Isn't it about time you got around to. . . ?"

Tears flowed in silent sadness as I watched the fire die.

Suddenly Harvey charged out of the bathroom with a sly, I've-got-you-now look on his face that startled me.

"You're supposed to be the literary one, aren't you? Haven't you heard, 'Laugh and the world laughs with you, cry and you cry alone'?" He headed for the bedroom, heh, heh, hehing to himself.

I wiped my face. I don't remember crying again until I lay on the dock that night, wet and weeping, with those comforting words wracking through me.

Stay, let me weep while you whisper,
  Love paid the ransom for me.

As time went on, the children brought their friends to the house less and less.

And they came to me more and more with their concerns and delights. Like the weekend Grace was named Most Valuable Player at a basketball championship game.

"Good for you. Congratulations." I was thrilled for her, adding, "You must tell your father tomorrow."

"Why?" she asked. "He never lets us finish a sentence. Someday he's going to wake up and notice that nobody talks to him. and he won't even know why."

What she said was the truth, and I felt concern for Harvey. But I said nothing.

Sunday, April 7
Joanna, I've done some reading and much thinking. Why do I remain silent when I am aware?

Because I know what is expected of a Christian wife.

Wives, submit yourselves unto your own husbands (Eph. 5:22).

Wives, be in subjection to your own husbands. . . . Even as Sara obeyed Abraham, calling him lord (1 Peter 3:1, KJV).

Wasn't complaining of one's husband petty and un-Christlike?

Wasn't a husband special in God's order?

This is what we were given in premarriage counseling from the church and from a book recommended by the church office: *The Home, Courtship, Marriage and Children* by John R. Rice.

> *A man is a somebody!*
> *For the husband is the head of the wife, even as Christ is the head of the church, and he is the saviour of the body. Ephesians 5:23*
>
> *God's inspired Word tells us that the man is the image and glory of God: but the woman is the glory of the man. A man is like God in a sense that a woman is not like God. God is masculine.*
>
> *For example: God is always in the Bible called He, never she. He is called Father, never mother. Christ is called the man, not the woman. He is called Bridegroom, not bride, King not queen, Prophet not prophetess, Son not daughter.*
>
> *Christ was a man, a masculine man. His body was a man's body. His work was a man's work. His temptations a man's temptations.*
>
> *God would not have had the Bible so full of it if He did not want us to notice that Christ was a man, not a woman, and that man is therefore made in the image of God in a sense that cannot be true of woman.*
>
> *So in the home, man is the deputy of God.**

And that, Joanna, is what I expected Harvey to be when I said those words, "To love, to honor, and to obey,

---

* *The Home, Courtship, Marriage and Children,* John R. Rice, pp. 86, 87.

till death us do part." He gave me that book and under-lined parts in red for me to read with particular attention.

When we married, I was secretary at Christ's Church on the Hill and was deeply involved in the Christian Education department of the work, to which I contributed time, effort, food, and money. I expected to continue some interest in these areas after marriage. After all, the bulk of church workers are married women.

But shortly after we were married, Harvey came in one midmorning as I was putting the finishing touches to a chocolate cake for a missionary convention church supper that night.

"What, again? That's the third time this month you've taken food there."

Actually it was the third time in three months, but I didn't correct him. I didn't want an argument; I just wanted to get the cake I'd promised to the church on time.

"You're a married woman now — married to a work-ing man — not a free-spending, single girl any more! You shovel it out faster than I can bring it in. You can stop right now!"

So I did. But the embarrassment I suffered went on for a long time. I still blush at the sound of the words, "I'm sorry, I can't this time," or "Not this week. I just can't. I'm sorry."

*Every wife is to be subject to her husband as if he were the Lord Jesus.**

So I was a loyal subject, even when surprised at the areas in which this "lord" I'd married required subjection.

I've always been an interested reader of the Bible. Sometimes I find a Scripture mentally stimulating and follow an idea through into concordance, dictionaries, and commentaries, making notes as I go. Often I use these later in teaching or story-writing.

* Ibid., p. 89.

One evening when I was in the midst of one of these read-and-search sprees, Harvey came in and demanded to know how come I wasn't in bed. "Why do you think you got to read all the time? Don't you know you're a house-wife, not a schoolgirl?"

I replied that I was reading as a Christian, not as a schoolgirl, and I didn't know there was any age barrier to Bible study.

But Harvey seemed to feel there was a role barrier to it, and said so. "If some of you religious women running the church weren't so heavenly minded and paid a little more attention to your husbands, you might get them to do something in the church."

You see, Joanna, I took my marriage vows seriously, and the church's popular interpretation of them — sub-mission, subjection. So I quit reading my Bible when Har-vey was in the room. Gradually my thinking, writing, praying world completely separated from my relationship with Harvey, as different as the east is from the west, and never the twain shall meet. Only once in a while they did, and I always seemed to come out the loser.

Like the day Harvey met me in the college rotunda after a one-day writers' conference in Toronto. Spouses, not interested in writing, gathered there after their day of city shopping to meet conferees. One of the group, a soft-spoken, grey-haired gentleman said to Harvey, "Doesn't it make you feel humble to have such a talented wife?"

Harvey looked astounded, sputtered, then rallied. "I'd feel more humble if she'd stay home and mend my socks once in a while. Haw! Haw! Haw! Charity begins at home, you know. Heh! Heh! Heh!"

After that I limited my efforts to the church where I felt some family responsibility. But when Mark was born, I was so busy that even this became increasingly difficult.

During one pre-Sunday-school hassle, trying to keep a six-year-old boy clean while I fed and dressed the baby and

116

at the same time talked an eight-year-old girl out of her
school jeans and into her Sunday best, Harvey stormed
through. "What's all the racket about?"

"I'm teaching this morning. Wouldn't you know this
would be the morning everything happens to slow me
down?" I rushed past him with a soiled diaper, calling
back, "Just give me ten more minutes. If the car starts
OK, I'll have them all with me, and the house will be
quiet."

"Ten more minutes? It'll be quiet right now! Right this
minute, you hear!" Then he did a double take, noticing I
was dressed for church under a Mother Hubbard apron.

"Of course the car won't start! You didn't tell me you
wanted it. I put the battery on the charger in the basement,
so it'll start easier for me at midnight. Cold weather is hard
on the starting mechanism of a car. . . ."

I wished he had as much sympathy for the kids and me
as he had for that car, but I said, "The kids and I always go
to Sunday school. I'm teaching. I'm committed. I've got to
go."

"You don't do nothing, less I say so. And what I say is:

> Let your women keep silence in the churches, for it is not
> permitted unto them to speak, but they are commanded to
> be under obedience as also saith the law. And if they will
> learn anything let them ask their husbands at home, for it
> is a shame for women to speak in the church."*

But the shame I felt came from *not* speaking. A hot
pain shot up the back of my neck and settled into a tight,
pulsating band around my head. I felt it afresh every time
someone phoned to ask if I would speak at a missionary
meeting, Christian Business Women's, or World Day of
Prayer.

Reading the Scripture lost all comfort for me, for the
shame was there every time I read the parable of the tal-
ents, or such words as:

* 1 Corinthians 14:34, 35 KJV

No one who puts his hand to the plow and looks back . . . is
fit for the kingdom of God.*

Still, I worked as hard as I could to love, honor, and
obey.
A vow is a vow.

Tuesday, April 30
Joanna, I am amazed as the futility of it all unfolds
from those unfeeling years as I research my own thinking,
write to you, and read in the Scriptures and the behavioral
sciences.

But when the work and responsibilities of the home
increased with the birth of Andrew, and my only support
from Harvey consisted of the cash household allowance, I
became more alone and lonely and tried all the harder for a
fulfilling marriage.

Even when I doubted the rightness in some of Harvey's attitudes and judgments, I was alone with my
doubts. To talk it over with a Christian friend was out.
Harvey considered "chitty-chatting" on the phone about
anything on a par with gossip.

To talk to the pastor was out, for he considered wom-
en's complaints as rebellion against the God-ordered state
of marriage.

So I tried again to talk to Harvey. And the conversation included such gems of masculine understanding as —
"So everybody else at the church goes to Couples' Club.
Everybody else isn't on shift work. Anyway, it's not good
to be conformed, remember? Be not conformed."

And — "So you're stuck in the house with four kids
with the measles. You're not the first woman in the world
to have that happen to her. Can't you ever learn to be
content with the state you're in? If you think you're too
good to spend all your time being a mother to those kids,
then you shouldn't have got married."

* Luke 9:62 AMPLIFIED

And another time when I asked Harvey to stay with the two youngest so I could take the two older children Christmas shopping — "Me?" he said. "I'm not their mother."

"But you are their father. Why shouldn't a father stay with his children once in a while?"

"Well, you'll not tie any apron around me so you can trot off to town and spend money right and left just for junk. Christmas shopping — who needs it?"

I knew that Harvey didn't. He never shopped for anyone for Christmas, so I said, "The children. That's who!"

"Says you! Well, I say they don't. I'm not made of money. It's about time we got that straight. Weren't you ever taught Christians should endure hardness as good soldiers of Jesus Christ? Nobody leaves this house to go Christmas shopping."

I swallowed a silent scream, *How un-Christian can you get in the name of caring for your children?* I watched him troop to the garage, thinking, *Hardness from unbelievers, yes. From the world, yes. But, Lord, must one expect this in a Christian marriage? Can't a girl expect some understanding, some tenderness, some sharing, some giving? Lord, if not for me, for the children?*

But I knew then that if there was to be any giving for the children or any Christmas ever, it wouldn't be from their father. I'd better get busy about it as best I could.

The children and I sat around the circular kitchen table. Grace held Mark on her knee, and I held Andrew on mine, as we made our lists from the mail-order catalog.

It wasn't the same as the sights and sounds of the department stores decorated for Christmas, but afterward we made popcorn and taffy and strung lights and sang Christmas carols. When Grace and Jeremy had to go do their homework, I tucked the two youngest, then two and six, into bed and read them the Christmas story.

I remember looking at them and thinking, *My chil-*

dren *will have some part of the traditional Christmas as long as I am alive.*

Joanna, every time the kids recall the good things of Christmases past, they always mention our night of catalog shopping, how they talked over everything in the wish book and ordered right under each other's noses, yet how on Christmas morning each was completely surprised by the secret thoughtfulness of their meager gifts to each other.

As time went on and the children grew older, I continued to obey and submit, to be subject, though I developed grave doubts as to the validity, even the Christianity, in it at times.

*Woman is the glory of the man, and the woman was created for the man. This is God's plan and it is good, good for the happiness and welfare of both men and women.**

Harvey gloried in hauling home old motors and towing old cars into the yard to tinker on. When working the night shift, as he did so much, he had a lot of time in daylight hours. So I towed old cars home for him while he steered the second car. I sat bundled in blankets with children desperately in need of going to the bathroom, shivering on my knee, while Harvey tried to start his newly acquired prize to take it home under its own power. When six months' pregnant, I changed tires on the freeway with two children in the car. I've driven by the letter of the law so the police wouldn't stop me and run a check on the license plates, because I suspected Harvey had switched them or borrowed them from some other vehicle.

Harvey's only answer to my question about it was, "Don't ask. What you don't know won't hurt you." Somehow I didn't think the police would accept that.

Living in such fear is good for the welfare of whom?

In the very nature of men and women, God has written the fact that man should be head of the home and wives
*Home, Rice, p. 104.

> secondary to them in authority, and subject to them. To change this order violates the laws of nature as well as the command of God. This is why modern homes are unhappy and cannot have the favor of God.*

Joanna, all of my instincts cried out, *Who can be happy living with selfishness, tyranny, hard-heartedness?* If ordained of God, as some writers suggest, it still violates all who must live with such. Do not I have some rights as a human being, if not as a wife? Didn't the Spirit of the Lord strike Ananias's wife, Sapphira, dead along with him — equal responsibility for the sin of the household?

But all of the church's marriage counseling was well-ingrained in my mind. I have a good memory for what I read. And what I forgot, Harvey never failed to remind me of.

> Every time God gives orders to husbands and wives about their treatment of each other in the Bible, He speaks to wives first, then husbands.
> When He commands fathers and children about their duties to each other, He commands children first, and then fathers. He commands servants first, then masters, subjects first, then rulers. God wants no excuses . . . for a child who does not want to obey his father, or a wife who does not want to obey her husband.**

So often when I've heard him scolding the children harshly about the way they piled wood, or raked the lawn, or carried in groceries, I'd think, *If only Harvey were different, the parent-child relationship could be such fun.* I wasn't questioning his right to give orders, just the unreasonableness of his manner.

> God expects women to feel their duty to obey their husbands good or bad, saved or unsaved. Nowhere in the Bible is a wife's duty to her husband conditioned on the kind of character he has, or the way he treats her.

> This divine order in giving commands to men and women

* Ibid., p. 104.
** Ibid., p. 105.

could not be an accident, but is evidently meant to leave those who should obey without an excuse for not doing so.

Sometimes I feel my marriage situation is nothing more than church-sanctioned chauvinism — it sets Harvey free to be selfish, and makes me feel guilty for it.

*Wives be obedient to, submit to, be subject to, even reverence your husband. If women cared about what God expects their attitude to be toward their husband. . . .***

I cared. Oh, Joanna, how I cared!

I obeyed all those years, always attempting to walk around any real confrontation with Harvey, except when his anger threatened violence to one of the children. Then I acted instinctively. I'd snatch the child away and stand in its place, blurting out my one line of resistance.

Oh, no, you don't . . . over my dead body. . . .

I loved, I honored, I obeyed, and I walked to the dock and tried to drown myself.

So what can I tell my daughter when she looks at me with the idealism of adolescence and the honesty of a realist and asks, "Are all Christian marriages this awful?"

I rushed in with, "Oh, Grace, don't make a judgment on Christianity for the failure you see in me, in my marriage — "

"Oh, mom, it's not just you. I hear. I see. Girls talk." And then she told me: "Mom, Wanda's dad is not anything like father. He's involved in Christian work. But Wanda's mother is a doormat that says 'Welcome' — to her husband's boys' brigade, and his Sunday school class, and the board of deacons. . . .

"Judy's dad is a lawyer, goes all out to help teen-agers hung up on drugs. But Judy's mother is a one-line record — 'Yes, Ron. You're right, Ron. This is a recording.'

"Sue Martin's dad is choir director and leader of a

* Ibid.
** Ibid.

male quartet. Sue's mother is a mirror that says, 'You're the handsomest of them all.' ''

I didn't have the nerve to ask, Joanna, but she told me anyway.

"And you're a clothesline for father to air out his pet peeves on and to pin all his bad temper to. I can hear, and I can see, mom. I know you work two shifts to his one. You take the blame for everything he doesn't like and you live on sufferance. Mom, is this all there is to a *Christian* marriage? The big lottery of life — a few win, but a lot more lose. And you're stuck with a loser for life!''

Oh, Joanna, Joanna, what could I say? Doesn't a Christian marriage have anything more than this to offer? I obeyed all the rules for a successful Christian marriage, and there is nothing more for me.

And yet, I can't let Grace pick up her father's no-value system for women. It's not right. Women have souls too.

I can't remain silent much longer. I obeyed all the rules, and the rules don't work.

Allison

Chapter 14

Evanston, Illinois
Sunday, May 12

My dear Allison,

You did not obey *all* the rules.

You obeyed *half* of them. The other half aren't yours to obey. They are your husband's responsibility. Look at them. I did. Although it took me a week to track down some of the fundamentalist writings on marriage you've mentioned.

Read the advice to husbands.

Likewise, ye husbands, dwell with them [wives] according to knowledge, giving honour unto the wife, as unto the weaker vessel, and as being heirs together of the grace of life.*

Live considerately with [your wives], with an intelligent recognition . . . honoring the woman . . . joint heirs of the grace (God's unmerited favor).**

* 1 Peter 3:7 KJV
** 1 Peter 3:7 AMPLIFIED

123

124

To me, this doesn't seem to indicate the same master-servant relationship that has been suggested, or should I say perpetrated, toward you. Though, in fairness to those writers who raise the man to this high status of full authority over the wife and children, I must say that they also give man the added responsibility. This sounds like logical regimentation as in an army, although it doesn't seem to have much to do with the marriage relationship as seen in 1 Peter 3:7.

However, even the most fundamental fundamentalists do not suggest a man should take authority *without* responsibility. I was about to say this is tyrannical or dictatorial, but actually it is childishness. Even dictators and tyrants take some responsibility — only very young children take none.

> *God will hold you more accountable for the happiness of the home than the wife. From the Bible standpoint there is no getting out of this truth.** *

And again:

> *Husbands, love your wives, and be not bitter against them (Colossians 3:19 KJV).*
> *No matter how much your wife has failed, be not bitter against her. You are to love your wife, as Christ loved the church. You are to be long-suffering as He is long-suffering toward us.*
> *You are to be forgiving, as He is forgiving.*
> *You are not to hold grudges, not to hold resentment, not to be bitter. For a husband to be bitter against his wife is a sin.***

Render unto the wife due benevolence (1 Cor. 7:3).

My dear Allison, in this past year we've shared, by mail, Scripture-talk, woman-talk, family-talk. Though I've never met them, your children are full-blown personalities in my mind's eye.

You, I've met. I know your measurements and have

*Home, Rice, p. 116.
** Ibid., p. 125.

rejoiced in your consistent weight loss. Yet I feel my mental image of you is less accurate than my image of your children, for it remained that of the gentle, willowy girl I once met at the spring conference of '65, autographing her pretty, romantic novels about lovely heroines.

Or it did, until I read those bitter-sad lines in your last letter: "I loved, I honored, and I obeyed, and I walked to the dock and tried to drown myself." Suddenly my mind-picture of you flipped to a new frame, one that corresponds with the dialogue I've been receiving from you.

For a second I wondered, who is this look-you-straight-in-the-eye person with need for honesty, staring at me from the pages of your last letter?

She is a shirttail cousin to that tender-hearted girl who once had to have everything she wrote so pretty-pretty or it couldn't be labeled Christian. And if she didn't feel good about it, she labeled it bad and pretended the feelings weren't there.

This girl I'm seeing now knows that Christian faith does not deny feelings, but accepts them, awful as they sometimes are, and looks beyond them to the Lord for whatever is lacking.

Remember? About a year ago you first wrote: "I can't characterize that girl who tried to drown herself, because I don't know her." Again: "She's some distant cousin whom I haven't met since childhood." And again: "I've role-played so long that I can't find the real me."

Allison, you can now! The letters I'm getting are now written by that girl grown up!

That's right! The fat-cow armor you grew to protect that little girl from a world she couldn't face is gone. And that girl who recognized courage and a sense of humor in a horse and sobbed tears is alive and well! A thinking, feeling, worshiping being, and still growing.

Your measurements tell me that you are no longer a fat cow.

And now your words say it too: "My children have souls. I cannot let my daughter pick up a no-value system."

You are back on the real battleground now, Allison.

For we wrestle not against flesh and blood, but against principalities, against powers, against the rulers of the darkness of this world, against spiritual wickedness in high places (Eph. 6:12 KJV).

When we let the stress of daily life shift our eyes away from the real battle, the battle between Satan and the Lord for the souls of humanity, it is the natural instincts of loyal women to cover for their husbands or their children, or even themselves, in areas of weakness.

When your husband, through preoccupation or boorishness or whatever, didn't appreciate the loving creativity which you'd poured into your culinary arts, you sat down and ate twice as much and probably in a doubly proper manner.

I have known both men and women who, on finding an insensitivity to Christian things in their spouses, tried to compensate — to have religion for two. The jest "Put in a good word for me" popularizes this idea.

Mothers who cover for their children's wrongdoings are the bane of justice in juvenile courts and a thorn in the flesh of churches. For sin, when covered, festers and hurts the whole body of believers — sooner or later.

What can you tell your daughter?

The truth. The rules for a happy Christian marriage only work when *all* the rules are followed. Half is never enough. There isn't anything else but honesty.

But to you, Allison, my friend, there is so much I want to say. At the risk of sounding like some writers, with a Scripture verse for every idea, I suggest you read John 1:16 in all the translations you have. "Grace for grace." In the Amplified — "For out of His fullness we were all supplied with — one grace after another."

It's because the rules don't work unless *all* are kept that God gave us grace at such a terrible sacrifice — but in Christ He did give. Annie Johnson Flint says it better than I can:

> He giveth more grace when the burdens grow greater,
> He sendeth more strength when the labors increase;
> To added affliction, He addeth His mercy,
> To multiplied trials, His multiplied peace.
>
> His love has no limit; His grace has no measure;
> His power no boundary known unto men.
> For out of His infinite riches in Jesus,
> He giveth and giveth and giveth again.

Allison, there is grace for you. The saving grace of "Love paid the ransom" for you. And added to that, there is the grace to make you whole. One grace after another for the thinking, feeling, worshiping being. So think it, sense it, pray it.

"Saving my soul, making me whole."

With you in this prayer,
Love,

Joanna

Chapter 15

Dear Joanna,

As has happened so often before, Joanna, in trying to explain my quandary to you, I end up explaining it to myself — somewhat.

I can see now that I tried to live up to the church's expectations of me as a young married woman, only to find this in conflict with my husband's expectations of me as a Christian wife. So out of loyalty to the love, honor, and obey of the marriage vows, I stopped trying to relate to the body of believers outside the home.

But that did not quell the conflict for me either, for I was more alone than ever — mentally and spiritually. I ate to fill a hunger, but all I got was the added calories. Then I despised my soulless existence and wanted to die.

Now that I've reestablished my claim to "Love paid the ransom for me" and acted on the fact that there can be no exchange for a soul, I can feel again. I feel alive unto God.

In my children I have a nonphysical or spiritual work right within the home raising them in the nurture and admonition of the Lord. So even the physical is more alive. I can feel!

As I worked in the garden this spring, I was no longer insulated with the gross layer of fatty fluid I perspired through last year, so I felt the sun warming my skin. When I knelt to plant greens, beans, and peas, I felt the sinewy movement of muscles in my calf, thigh, and buttocks, muscles I'm sure were once immobilized in my obesity.

Thirty-seven-and-a-half pounds off in almost eight months isn't such a rapid loss, but it leaves me only nine more pounds to go! Even my shoes, partial denture, and glasses seem too big for me. Never in all my life have I bought three new bras in one year. Size-wise I've had to. I take in the too-big ones for wearing around home, but I buy to fit for dress wear. I'm teaching again! Just a six-week elective in a Bible class, but it is a returning to church life for me.

As much as I enjoy teaching Bible, nothing is as mind-expanding as listening and watching, actually seeing one's own children as thinking, feeling, worshiping beings — completed entities.

What a stretching of the moral fiber in a mother this birth of a child is! And knowing each as a believing, reborn child of God — shattering and awe-filling. Parent to a completed child!

Joanna, it is hard to explain, but once I was overworked and overburdened, running as hard as I could to care for them physically. Yet when I added to that the responsibility of nurturing the souls and spirits (minds and wills) of these individuals, the task was less, the burden lighter.

Oh, I still run, but I accomplish more. And what is so wonderful, I *feel* some sense of accomplishment.

First Corinthians 9:24-27 which had shamed me so is now a delight. But like a boxer, I know I must continue to discipline my body, to subdue it, that after proclaiming to you my present goal, I might not let myself become a counterfeit again. If I just *think* I have control and stop looking at the honest facts (counting my calorie intake), my control slips.

Something beautiful began to happen as my extra poundage started to melt away — my armor-coated role of mother started to disintegrate, too. My relationship with the children is more flexible, because it is more than physical work now. We stop for play. A few minutes to take basket shots — a ring Jeremy mounted on our flagpole. Or to pitch baseball with the younger ones — the older ones are too swift for me yet. And we play mental games at night, if we can manage the time amid homework and everything else — Scrabble, charades, and word association games from the Scripture. Though not of school age yet, Andrew is learning words rapidly, and teamed with Mark the two make a fourth player who needs no handicap from anyone.

Monday, July 15

This year every berry-picking trip is a picnic. I leave Harvey's lunch prepared in the frig. Also Jeremy's, for he's haying for a farmer on the next road. Ours I pack in an extra berry bucket which we bring back filled with big blackberries oozing rich, purple-red juice.

We are freezer-packing the fruit for winter, but our thoughts and feelings of these trips into the bush are very much unfrozen. The sting of cane-scratched hands and arms, the itch of mosquito bites, and the sense of loss in an upset pail of berries. The fun of finding a killdeer nest, a pair of playful coons, and an unhurried, dignified skunk, to whom we gave the right of way and only laughed about after the white-striped lady in question was well out of earshot.

And our conversation, whether at work or play, is a discovery of ourselves and each other.

Yet for all of this, I soon felt that something was lacking in this joyful summer. So I began looking for some planned Scripture reading for the children.

Family devotions is one of the rules for a successful Christian family that we never managed with any kind of "good vibrations" (Grace's word), for it so often ended in a "flap" (Jeremy's word).

In our last such bad scene of several years ago, Jeremy was praying when Harvey broke in — "Speak up, kid, I can't hear you."

Without lifting his head, Jeremy answered his father — "I'm not talking to you. I'm sure God can hear me all right."

Thus our family Bible-reading ended in a tirade against mumbling in prayer like the heathen do, and talking in words not understood by man, and so on.

With the breakdown of the family altar into just one more time for parent rule and the laying down of the law, I set it aside too, for the sake of peace in the family. But now a longing for some home Scripture study for these thinking, feeling, worshiping children haunted me.

How silly sensible people are sometimes, Joanna!

Because my children are thinking, feeling, worshiping beings, they don't need any person to act as intermediary for them. To do so would be role-playing the work of Jesus Christ to them.

Joanna, Joanna, when will I ever learn that it's not for me to decide right and wrong and lay blame or pick it up for every "flap" of family life. It's my task to feed their minds.

I looked over devotional materials for each child at his

or her own age level and decided on Scripture Union Bible
Reading Notes as a thought-starter for them. I looked at the
filled-in form in my hand and knew Harvey would say,
"Get the family plan. It's cheaper. We're a family, aren't
we?"

So I left the order on my desk for a couple of days,
wondering. When I was making up the Sunday church
offering envelope, I noticed it and thought, *If that was
Scripture for any other needy child, I wouldn't hesitate at
the individual cost.* Why should I with my own? Their
souls are equally valuable.

I mailed the order on the way to church.

When the booklets came, each child took his to his
room. I'd coached myself not to question them about it,
knowing that any spiritual work must be God-prompted. I
used mine daily and left it in a Bible on the telephone table
available for Harvey.

Then one night I was typing in the office when I heard
conversation across the upstairs hallway. Mark and Andrew were supposed to be sleeping, and I had just started
up the stairs when I recognized Jeremy's exaggerated
whisper. "Hey, Grace I just found out the answer to father's
favorite put-down — 'If you're so smart, why aren't you
rich?' It's in today's reading, Ecclesiastes 9:10-12."

I went back to the office and my letter to you, but first I
looked up the reference.

> The race is not to the swift, nor the battle to the strong,
> neither yet bread to the wise, nor yet riches to men of
> understanding, nor yet favour to men of skill; but time and
> chance happeneth to them all.*

I smiled to myself over these two older children of
mine, but it was a sad smile for all that. So pleased with the
children, if only it wasn't their father. . . .

It was Andrew, the youngest, who loved his little book
best of all. He needed a lot of help, and he demanded it

* Ecclesiastes 9:11 KJV

regularly, every evening when the older ones started their homework. With pride and joy he did his homework. (He started kindergarten last week.) His childlike enjoyment of the Scripture stories is a wonderful way to put my day's effort into perspective and lay it to rest for the night.

Sunday, September 15

I intended to have this off to you before now, but the summer has been so busy — gardening, pickling, canning, packing for winter. And not the best time for dieting — so many fresh fruits and vegetables that taste so delicious in a cream sauce or topped with whipped cream. So now I must tighten up my self-discipline for the toughest stretch of dieting — to shed the last nine extra pounds before snowfall.

The children are continuing their Scripture-reading with enthusiasm. But not all of their candid conversations around their readings are comfortable. It takes an older child to question a mother to the quick the way Grace did the other day.

"Mother, he's so negative-negative-negative." Suddenly she turned to me. "Mother, why didn't you marry a Christian?"

"I did. He is. Or was. I thought he was." I sighed in frustration. "Grace, you know your father is a Christian?" And I was ashamed of myself for letting it come out as a question.

Grace shook her head, her long hair twitching at the end like Scout's tail when stalking through the leaves in the lawn to catch a mouse or mole. "Mom, I know he doesn't drink, doesn't smoke, doesn't dance — but *he doesn't do anything else either!*"

"Child, child —" I sympathized with her as I mentally rushed to Harvey's defense. "He wasn't always the way you see him now. He works hard. Shift work isn't easy —"

"Oh, mother, I'm not Mark or Andrew. It's me — Grace. I'm sixteen years old! I can add two and two and get four, every time. I can read too. I've read most of the library books you've brought home this past year.

"The more he yells, the more I go to my room and read. I used to keep romances under my mattress, but the philosophy and psychology you're reading is far more fascinating. I'm not a child any more, mom!"

I could see she wasn't. As tall as I am, slender, yet rounded, a pretty young lady in spite of faded jeans and an out-of-shape T-shirt.

Just then she flung her arms around my neck in a childlike bear hug. "Mom, oh, mom. Don't back away on me now! Don't hide behind some silly rule. Don't leave me alone — mom, I love you!"

All of her sophistication suddenly disappeared in a flood of tears as her words tumbled out, "Mom, you taught me to be considerate and honest and fair — don't change all that now, mom?"

Then with a sideways, sad grin she went on, "I got such a kick out of you and that cauliflower. I didn't have the heart to tell you I thought it was a nothing-tasting vegetable. That silly vegetable and your diet is the first time you've stood up to father and acted on the facts according to you!

"Mom, I'd go to the garden and eat worms if it'd help you to stop taking his put-downs." She was crying great childish sobs.

"Every time I hear one of his favorites — 'Be content. Be not conformed. What more do you want, you got a roof over your head and food on the table? If you're so smart, why aren't you rich? You never had it so good. Endure hardness.' — I want to scream, 'Liar, liar, pants on fire!'"

She gulped for air and sighed. "But that's childish, and I'm not a child any more. So, mom, I've got to talk adult to you.

"Mom, stop being a lie-ee!"

I didn't understand what she meant, but the genuine feeling in her broken voice and the deep concern on her tear-smeared face left me speechless. I blew my nose, wiped my eyes, and waited for Grace to do the same.

"Mom, father is always coming out with his pet statements which sound true, but he uses them in defense of an untrue situation. Like, 'I work shift work.' True, he does. But the false inference here is, 'Woman, you don't work shift work' — or, 'You don't work.'

"But I know better, mom. When you're up nights with babies and sick kids or late suppers for the shift worker in the family, you always work the day shift too. I remember once when Jeremy had scarlet fever, you never went to bed for seven nights — and you still did the day work too. But father slept in the daytime, because he *worked shift work.*

"Even a kid can see shift work is a cinch compared to 24-hour duty, 7 days a week. Is it any wonder I want to scream, 'Liar, liar, pants on fire' every time he comes out with that one?"

Joanna, the words that poured out of this oldest child of mine shocked me into total, listening silence.

"A liar is one who tells a lie.

"A lie-ee is one who accepts that lie."

I was astounded by her simple logic, and asked meekly, "Did you figure this out by yourself?"

"Aunt Rita — "

"You've discussed your father with Aunt Rita?"

"Oh, mom, don't go all stuffy on me. Aunt Rita's known him longer than we have. But I didn't talk to her about that. It was the day I was voted the most valuable player at the basketball championship game. That Annabell Sykes shot off her mouth about, *'It must be nice having an aunt on the Awards Committee!'*

"You know the kind of snide remarks some people make to discount anything anyone else has which they haven't. But if it'd been hers, suddenly inflation would set in.

"Annabell, I'm used to," Grace explained with re-signed sportsmanship. "What really bugged me was that Jamie Johnson agreed with Annabell, and Jamie is a super player himself — really knows the game. I was snorting steam when Aunt Rita came along to ask me about you and your diet. So I told her about Annabell.

"Aunt Rita looked at me for a minute as if sizing me up to see if I was old enough to be told the truth. Then she let me have it.

" 'It is true that your aunt is on that committee. But the *whole* truth is that you won that trophy without my vote. When you were nominated, I disqualified myself on the grounds of possible prejudice *for*.'

" 'You see, Grace, to keep on being a winner, you've got to learn — *never let a liar or a lie-ee get you down*. Their opinion is not valid criticism. Annabell doesn't hustle her bustle enough on the basketball floor to be voted most valuable anything. And Jamie is all the bigger lie-ee for accepting or agreeing with her not wholly true statement!' "

Joanna, I was beginning to understand, but Grace wasn't finished with me yet.

"A few nights after that, mom, when father was expounding on 'I'm the one that brings home the pay check,' I saw what Aunt Rita meant.

"Father does bring home the pay check — true. But the full situation is — the family still wouldn't be fed, clothed, and clean without your work, mom. The only time anyone notices your work is when it *isn't* done. Like, 'Where are my socks? Aren't my jeans washed? Cookie jar empty again?' Right, mom?

"You do repetitive work without any resale value, for what you do today will be consumed tonight and will have to be repeated tomorrow. But that is no reason you should be put down for it. We couldn't survive without your work, even if it has no cash value in this situation."

"Grace, you've been doing a lot of reading and a lot of thinking."

She nodded slowly. "You haven't answered my question yet. How come you married a man like father?"

"Grace — " I swallowed a growing lump of uncertainty. This was no child to be brushed off with excuses, platitudes, or even rules. It had to be the truth, the whole truth, and nothing but the truth. But the truth I didn't know.

"I've asked myself a lot of futile questions over this past year, my child. Whose fault? Why did I do wrong? Why is this happening to me? Where did I go wrong?"

The boys and Scout chose that moment to come bounding in with their tongues hanging out for a drink. So I promised Grace I'd give her a whole-truth answer as soon as I found it.

You see, Joanna, I no longer hold any illusion that all is well on this *Christian* marriage scene. In fact, as the children grow older and their logic and honesty and understanding increase, there are moments when the tension and conflict take on the feeling of an armed camp or a psycho ward.

I can no longer stretch myself around the children's need to know Christian truth and Harvey's need to use half-truths.

Sometimes I wonder if everything will blow up in my face.

Wednesday, September 18

I can see it now.

What Grace said to me is true, and the subtlety of it astounds me. As much as such words as liar, lie-ee, false trust, and perverted faith stick in my craw, the fact remains that the real enemy in the church-blessed married state, as in anything else, is Satan.

The innocent party accepts a half-truth given and picks up the guilt for the untruth perpetrated. Then Satan can sit back and say to himself, "Ha! Ha! I got you both, liar and lie-ee, and I did it all by using nothing but the best — the Scriptures — with a little help from the rules of the church subculture."

And because I'd lost sight of my real adversary, Joanna, I went blissfully on assuming that because I'd obeyed the rules like a good girl should, I could overcome by being a good girl — a good cook, a good housekeeper, a good wife, a good mother — and it would all add up to a good marriage.

And I ended up at the dock, still being a good girl, accepting guilt for having sold my soul for a roof over my head and food on the table. The mess of pottage, and death the end due a life of emptiness.

Now I know what you meant by the "good little girl syndrome."

But I still can't find the answer to Grace's questions, for the fact remains — I did obey all the rules *before* marriage too.

1. Christians should marry only Christians.

I met Harvey at young people's meetings in church. We attended church regularly, took part in all church activities. In fact the church was the center of our being together.

2. Christians should have an honorable length of engagement.

I knew Harvey as one of the church young people for five years or more. He was in the army when I was in college. Some time after I became secretary to Dr. Pickering, Harvey started coming to church in civilian clothes. As our friends married and the Christian group had parties and presentations for them, Harvey and I saw more of each other. We were officially engaged six months before we married.

3. Christians should have a public wedding with Christian emphasis.

We had a church wedding, white dress and veil. After the reading of the vows, we knelt at the altar in a personal commitment of dedication before all our relatives and friends. Mom and dad were still alive then.

4. A successful marriage should look forward to the blessing of children.

I'd prayed much about marriage. I wanted to live in God's will for me. I had no fear of being an "old maid," for I had a fulfilling job in the church. Yet I suppose I considered the job of wife and mother in a Christian marriage as a higher calling, just as the church culture does. I certainly didn't foresee myself dropping completely out of Christian work and church activities. Church work was still a central part of the lives of Christian couples I knew, even after they had small children.

5. A successful marriage should accept a biblical standard for the marriage.

It was Harvey who gave me the books on Christian marriage. We agreed on its scriptural basis, as we agreed on everything — before we were married.

Joanna, if we agreed on everything before we were married, why is there no agreement, no unity, no companionship now?

As I ask myself the same questions all over again, I wonder why the Lord let me go this way? I looked to Him for guidance.

Wherever the fault lies, it isn't with the Lord. That is probably the only thing I know for sure right now.

I used to go through days of dark self-questioning; then I'd try to talk to Harvey about it, about how frustrated I felt in marriage. I'd pour out my desire to be a good wife, a good mother, a good Christian, trying to reach some spiritual understanding to fill the nothingness in our relationship.

But I always ended up accepting the blame for Harvey's fatigue in his job, for his ill temper with me, and for his feelings of poverty. And I'd try all the harder to remove first one source of his annoyance and then another.

Joanna, I believed in the happiness of a Christian in marriage and the institution of the family, and I kept on trying.

Now Grace's questions rankle the edges of my mind, again probing backward into my years of futile trying for happiness, with just as futile a search for answers.

I looked everywhere, including old snapshots taken before marriage, and wedding pictures, and snaps of the older children before Mark and Andrew were born. My camera broke, and I only have snaps of them which Rita took from time to time.

As I held a picture of Harvey in my hand, all of nineteen years of age, in uniform, I wished that Grace could somehow know what he was like then.

Golden Boy, my apartment roommate called him. Six feet tall, slim, with golden brown skin and blond hair — Golden Boy suited him.

Joanna, even then I wasn't totally unaware of Harvey's personality. I knew he was shy, lacking in polish and social initiative. But when he made a faux pas, I'd think, *If it wasn't for my mother, would I be any better?* I knew Harvey and his sisters had been raised by his father, a pensioner.

And we did go places together then — youth rallies, church-sponsored camping trips. He brought small, appropriate gifts and Christmas presents.

I know Grace would find that hard to believe, knowing that I wrap presents for myself and put them under the tree in order not to diminish the enjoyment the younger ones have in their giving and getting. He doesn't know when my birthday is. And the children have ceased to remind him since he "blew up" at Grace over Mother's Day, when she asked him why he never bought me a Mother's Day gift like the fathers of her friends did for their wives.

"Why should I buy her a Mother's Day present? *She's not my mother!*"

Grace reacted with all the aplomb of an eight-year-old, which she was at that time. "She's my mother, and I'll get her a present, somehow!" And she did. A lovely picture of trilliums, violets, and a jack-in-the-pulpit — real ones, pressed under glass and framed. It soon discolored because the child didn't have drying materials, but I wouldn't trade it for a Rembrandt.

Maybe the real question is, Where does love go?

It wasn't all in my imagination. I do not believe H. L. Mencken who wrote, "Love is the triumph of imagination over intelligence," for I have these snaps, a diary, and the little gifts lovers give.

Harvey was shy, humble, willing to take a back seat, as he puts it. He had strength and manliness, agreeableness and tenderness.

Joanna, I tell you the truth, there were those things between us then.

But it is also true that love is gone now, for how else could Harvey be part and party of a lie against me?

Oh, I'm not condoning my being a lie-ee. But I was a lie-ee *for* him. I have never been *against* Harvey.

Joanna, tell me, Where does love go?

Lovingly,

Allison

Chapter 16

Dear Allison,

Our plans for a sabbatical have shaped up so rapidly I feel seasick, and sore — in the left arm from shots.

I am so glad for you that you have a daughter like Grace. Cherish her friendship. It takes a brave child to talk as straight as she did.

Steve had a phrase he used to come out with whenever I turned horrified maternal dignity on something he said: "Now, mother, am I your enemy because I tell you the truth?"

Allison, I've become very fond of you, as one does with a younger sister arriving later in life. And with the paradox that plagues all human relationships, because of my sisterhood to you I hesitate, and yet because of it I have to be as brave as our kids and talk adult to you.

I have no doubt that these things — quietness, willingness, agreeableness, humility, manliness, strength, and tenderness — were in your relationship with Harvey at one time.

And I also believe everything you have written of him as he is now, because I can feel the hurt in your words, without pride or anger or vindictiveness — just the hurting. Because of that, let me say this:

Quietness, when it has nothing valid to say, must shout all the louder for a hearing.

Willingness to "take a back seat" is sometimes a religious reason for letting the other fellow do the job.

Agreeableness can be a matter of having no opinion to offer. It has a bonus too, for if someone else makes the decisions, that someone else must take the responsibility for results.

Humility is a spiritual grace, true, but so easily used as a false front for laziness to develop any active spiritual graces.

Manliness, after courtesy is dropped, becomes chauvinism.

Strength, if self-centered, is bullheadedness.

Chauvinism could assume that tenderness is no longer needed when one can assert his marriage rights!

Where does love go?

My guess is, when the emotional energy of young love ebbs and is not replaced by the spiritual strength of charity as seen in 1 Corinthians 13, then love dies a natural death — leaving an emptiness.

Often the emptiness left by a dead love is soon filled with hate.

This is not a "Christian" situation for you, as that girl who wrote the lovely-Lorna type books would readily agree. But what she didn't know then was that Christians live in just these circumstances, and more often than some might think. And live quite successful Christian lives, too. For the happiness of a Christian is not dependent on circumstances without, but those within — the wholeness of the soul.

But such a circumstance requires the great grace of Acts 4:33, the life filled and indwelt by the Holy Spirit.

Allison, thank God that you do hurt!

For if you hurt and you know it, you're alive!

And I think that the inverse of that is true, too. If you hurt and you don't know it — you're dead. Such was the case when you walked to the dock.

And it could possibly be the case with Harvey right now. He must hurt, as alone as he is. And he doesn't seem to know it.

From what I can tell by the objectivity of distance, whatever caused Harvey's hurt seems to predate you. Thus, his hostility and withdrawal are probably not personally directed toward you. Maybe you could talk to his sister Rita. She appears able to cope with her past, which is the same as Harvey's.

Allison, there is healing in the Holy Spirit for the hurt one suffers. I know, for I carried a terrible hurt toward mission boards in general and one in particular for decisions made during a political upheaval and property destruction that left me widowed and alone, with two infants.

That may sound like a misnomer — alone with two children — but I'm sure you understand it can be more alone than alone, singularly.

I was widowed, in a foreign country, without funds, without a job, with two little boys, one two-and-half-years and the other three months old.

On the premise of John 1:16, I picked up my babies and went on living. I raised them alone to the ages of twelve and fourteen, when I married Tom, their stepfather.

Several times you said, "How could you know?" I know because I've been there — alone.

Only after I admitted all of my feelings to myself, and

then confessed them to the Lord with a willingness to accept those circumstances as within the permissive will of God (though I do not see such as any active willingness on His part), was I able to cope with the present.

Had I refused what the old saints call "the Balm of Gilead," I would have been of all people utterly alone. As it was, I found I could go on, one day at a time, knowing it was enough that my Savior died for me.

Years later I watched without rancor as my son returned to work not far from where his father was killed. And now Tom and I are going for a short term with great anticipation and joy — because there is healing in the Holy Spirit.

Who knows? Maybe we'll even retire there, if the Lord tarries.

When a person lets go of the past, it returns to eternity from whence it came and releases one to live the present. Since the future is still in His hands, one can cope with today. It is enough! That is not a pat phrase or a complaisant put-down.

It is enough that my Savior died for me!

As for Grace's question, "How come, mom?"

Allison, I hope you kept carbon copies as all good writers should. Check back to your conference notes. Find the point . . .

> The strength of the Christian philosophy lies in its potential for problem-solving in personal interaction. But writers, too often, turn that strength into a weakness.

Replace the word writers with Christians.

What I'm getting at, Allison, is the labeling of things as Christian and unchristian. You mentioned this concerning Harvey's attitude toward Rita — isn't it time we accepted people as they are? By their fruits you shall know them.

I couldn't agree more. To accept a label without tasting the fruit behind it leaves one open to prejudice.

In being a lie-ee, as your daughter so aptly put it, you were *prejudiced for*.

Check those old conference notes again:

> *Christ in one's character can resolve one's thinking, but embracing Christianity does not solve one's problems out of print, and cannot do so in print – honestly.*

And in some cases, it adds to it, as it did in yours.

You accepted the label *Christian* for Harvey, therefore he was *equal*. And you obeyed the rule, "not unequally yoked together."

But when two are yoked, yet operating on two different levels of responsibility, you've got a yoke that hurts — be it man, woman, or ox.

The weakness of the Christian life in any individual is not so much the level of intelligence, but the level of irresponsibility.

All that is adorable in a newborn baby — its utter helplessness, its complete dependency, its attention-getting trickery, even its demanding wail for food — is met by the caring mother with sympathy and urgent effort, because the baby cannot help himself.

But put these same attitudes into an adult who will not help himself, and you've got an abnormality, and very likely a lazy, insensitive, stupid, selfish, self-centered person. The older such a person gets, the worse it appears and the more problems it creates.

If mentally incapable, it's called retardation.

If spiritually incapable, it's called irresponsibility.

How can such a situation improve?

Change the level of one of the yoked.

This you tried. You accepted Harvey's level of thinking for you — and you walked to the dock.

Now the only other alternative you have is to pray to God for wisdom and guidance that Harvey may be prompted by the Holy Spirit to stand a little taller as a man and as a man of God.

First must come some awareness of how badly he's hurting, and then the why can emerge to the conscious thinking, if he is willing.

Keep those letters coming —

Praying with you, as one survivor for another,

Love,
Joanna

Chapter 17

Shale Bay, Ontario
Wednesday, October 2

Dear Joanna,

How glad we are for you and pray Godspeed to you. This is a returning. Yet as teacher to one's grandchildren, it is no journey into the past, but rather a trip for the future.

As always you've helped.

Prejudiced *for*. How ironic!

Oh, to have the gift He gives us, to see ourselves as others see us.

I've asked myself a hundred times, "How can Harvey be so *prejudiced against* me, us, the children and me?" I was never *against* him. Yet I *was* prejudiced — prejudiced for.

Prejudice: an opinion held in disregard of factors that contradict it. An unreasonable bias. To be biased or blinded.

This goes along with the old adage, "Love is blind." The narrowing down of one's vision to see certain acceptable facts, until it leaves one blind to all evidence *against*.

One night last week, after I'd put the younger boys to bed and settled myself in the office to write, Grace came in. (I began a new book the day Andrew started school.)

"Look, mom," she dropped a book on my desk. "Look at this chapter on 'Wives Obey Your Husbands.' See, mom, all the red underlining. Now see the instructions to husbands — no red underlining."

Oh, Joanna, Joanna, how blind can one be? Harvey underlined those portions before he gave me the book for the Valentine's Day before we were married. I wonder if he even read the instructions to husbands?

Grace tapped a knuckle against the hard book cover. "Mom, there's something that really bugs me about this — the writer's use of pronouns. He has this thing about the literal acceptance of the total masculinity of the Godhead — Father, Lord, Christ. He believes that God would not have the Bible so full of it if He did not want us to notice that Christ was a man, not a woman, and that man is therefore made in the image of God in a sense that cannot be true of woman.

"So that's his viewpoint, and he's entitled to that," Grace said matter-of-factly. "But at that point his logic breaks down, because I don't see any reference to the feminine pronouns in Scripture.

"Mom, if he holds to such a literal understanding of terms like this, where does this leave the men in the church era? If the church is the bride of Christ, does this leave the male sex out of the church age?"

I explained that I sometimes find truth more readily understood by dropping the pronouns altogether. Such as — humanity, made a little lower than the angels, yet through the redemption of Jesus Christ raised to sit in heavenly places in Christ Jesus. Heirs of God, joint-heirs of Jesus Christ.

Even when the gender is used as in Luke 13:11-13, where Jesus accepted a woman's faith, and in Matthew 9:20-22, where Jesus expected a woman to grow in her soul, and also in Matthew 15:28, where Jesus said a woman's only limitation is herself — there is evidence that Jesus directed this grace and favor of the Godhead not because she was woman, but because she was a human being.

He, Christ, is the same to man, woman, child, because He does not label us by our labeling system. He sees inside — the Lord looks on the soul.

"Grace, it is we humans who put labels on people. Because discernment takes effort and real insight comes only with the indwelling Spirit. It is so much easier just to slap on a label. Yet no good can ever come of discounting the possibility of sin — one has to try the spirit, one's own as well as others.

"Prejudice is faulty thinking — whether for or against."

How clearly I see it now, Joanna, after all these years. Too soon old we get, too late smart!

Friday, October 4

It is our Canadian Thanksgiving time again. This year I feel such thankfulness in my soul. I don't want it to be just another day with a lot of emphasis on food that could end up with Harvey haranguing one of us, or all, for something we couldn't foresee would upset him.

All of my efforts to take the alternate route around his anger are wasted and impossible — and negative thinking on my part. So I racked my brain for some positive way of celebrating Thanksgiving that would please Harvey.

Friends? We don't have any — not mutual friends. Harvey doesn't like my friends and acquaintances from church, school, and the neighborhood, and he likes their husbands less.

Harvey's friends? He's made a swap or a deal with most of them at some time, and they aren't so friendly any more.

His family? Gladys is the only one he can say anything nice about. I hesitate there, knowing how she bugs the kids, but decided to talk to them about it, explaining my reasoning.

Mark groaned, "Gross! She'll start in on *violence in hockey* and father will agree with her, and there goes the all-star team for me!"

I had to agree with him that there was that risk.

Jeremy suggested we all pray about it in our own Scripture reading time and then talk it over in a day or two. See how we felt then.

Mark agreed to that. "Maybe prayer is the secret weapon that can protect us from Aunt Gladys."

Grace reminded him that there wasn't anything secret about it. Christ explained it to His disciples nearly two thousand years ago. It has been in print continuously for hundreds of years — "Where two or three are gathered together in My name, there am I in the midst"*

Later the kids gave me their consensus: they promised to put their best foot forward for Aunt Gladys, Uncle Albert, cousins Randy and Danny *if* Aunt Rita came too. But they were careful to add, "Don't blame us if the whole thing bombs — you know father!"

I waited up for Harvey to come in off the midnight shift so I could talk to him about it, without the children around.

"I'm working four to midnight, remember?" he said.

"We could have a noon meal."

* Matthew 18:20 KJV.

He watched me suspiciously, then blinked and grinned. "If you're all that energetic, woman, to cook and clean for a gang, then you can act like a woman to a hungry husband."

"You've just had three chicken-salad sandwiches and apple pie, and — "

But Harvey wasn't smiling any more. That wasn't the appetite he meant. He grabbed me. "Got you this time!" He pulled me to him. "You think you're pretty clever, looking at me with those calf eyes and turning away every time — "

"Harvey, you're hurting me. Not like this. Harvey, love is not like this — "

"How long do you think you can put me off, woman? How long do you think I'll go on supporting you without asserting my marriage rights?"

After that walk to the dock, the pastor advised Harvey, "Don't bother her for a while. She's had a shock. Let her get her strength back."

For a few weeks it was wonderful to go to bed without wondering if two hundred pounds of sweating man would wrestle the flesh until he felt he'd acted like a man, then flop over and snore loudly.

"What makes you think you're too good to act like a woman?"

"Harvey, if you want me to act like a woman at night, why don't you treat me like one during the day? You show more gentleness to the dog than you do to me. You bark out orders as if I were your slave. You couldn't treat a cleaning lady or a garbage man the way you do me and expect them to go on working for you."

Silently I thought, *No wonder I've felt like a prostitute so often.* My dream of love, honor, and obey turned into a nightmare, "The Rape of the Cleaning Lady."

"You're so clever with words, you just call it whatever you want to." Deliberately he took his pink pay check out of his back pocket, signed it, refolded it, and left it sticking out of his shirt pocket. "Now, are you going to come to bed and do your duty as a wife, or aren't you?"

"Do I have any choice?" I asked.

"Now, what kind of a stupid question is that? Of course you have a choice. You decide to be a wife, or else you explain to the kids why their mother has no money for food or fuel."

I looked around the kitchen, thinking, *I guess it is a choice or sorts.* Not a love and marriage choice as I had understood it, or a Christlike, caring attitude of a Christian spouse, but a choice none the less — no sex, no money.

Harvey has a favorite saying he used to ward off any request for help I made to him when the children were small: "You're not the first woman — "

I cradled my hands around the still-warm kettle, thinking, *I guess I'm not the first woman to come to this.*

Sarah and the Egyptian Pharaoh. Esther and the Persian king.

In the morning when I found Harvey's check where he'd tossed it on the kitchen counter, I wept. Not for myself, but for Harvey. I longed to say, "Harvey, I'm not your enemy. I'm not against you."

But I couldn't. To Harvey, something felt wrong in our marriage relationship. To his reasoning, it couldn't be him, so it had to be me.

Harvey seemed surprised when I went ahead with Thanksgiving plans, but no more irritable than if I hadn't. And it was the same when I agreed to teach another six-week elective at Bible school.

I expected a big explosion, but if he heard me, he never let on.

Joanna, he is really no more difficult when I do the things I once gave up than when I didn't, for the sake of peace in the family — a peace that never came.

All those years I wasted, trying out of Christian graciousness of wife for husband to walk around his "mad."

Being prejudiced for, I took whatever triggered the blow-up as the reason for it, when it was only the unreal reason. The real reason seems to be anger caged within Harvey. And it seems that his hostility, or anger, or whatever has nothing to do with us, the kids and me, except as we are a dumping ground.

Even the kids sense this.

The other night, Mark came in from the garage where he'd gone to tell his father the price of ice-time for his hockey team this fall. He said to Jeremy in passing, "My father is the most even-tempered man I know — always mad about something!"

Monday, October 14

Thanksgiving day dawned brilliantly. Shafts of sunlight shot through the early morning mists, spotlighting the bush surrounding our horseshoe-shaped village like an open treasure chest of color. Ruby maple leaves and emerald pines, both etched with diamondlike dew and set in a background of bronzed oaks and golden poplars.

Though slightly nervous over what I had started, I watched a few minutes and saw rainbows in the rising mists.

This is the day the Lord hath made. I will rejoice and be glad!

Rita came early, parked her Vette well off the driveway "out of reach of any backyard mechanics who might be around today."

"Ally, you're really something!" She hugged me. "You took it all off in one year — you look fabulous!"

She peeled potatoes, kidded the younger boys as they set the table, talked school with the older ones, and asked Harvey how the new government budget hit him.

When she got little response from him, she went on helping as happily as if he had answered her kindly.

I was pleased to see Harvey had put on a good pair of

156

slacks with a shirt and tie. But when he headed for the garage in them, I wondered if it was such a good idea after all.

"Ally," Rita whispered out of earshot of the kids. "You take Harvey too seriously. If he throws a temper tantrum like a child, then treat him as you would a child. If he pouts like a hyper teen-ager, then give it no more credence than you would that. Call it what it is, treat it accordingly, then go on about your work. Goodness knows with an eight-room house, big garden, and four kids, you've got enough!"

Later she said, "Don't write narrative for his dialogue. You know, 'This is your father speaking. This is the head of the house talking.' Let it stand on its own merits — or demerits. You're wasting your ability writing story transitions to prepare the kids for Harvey's put-downs like — 'Women should never have been given the vote. And women in pants are the ruination . . .' etc., etc."

Then the Andersens arrived.

Gladys hadn't been in the front door five minutes before she began unfolding to us her long-suffering with music teachers. Each time Gladys turned to ask, "Isn't that right, Albert?" the boys, nine-year-old Randy and eleven-year-old Danny, edged closer to the back door.

"Albert! You stop encouraging the boys in backyard rowdiness. It'll be the ruination of their hands. We've got enough athletes in the family now, goodness knows!" She glowered at Rita, muscle-taut and sleek in a camel-colored pantsuit, busily showing Grace how to fold a napkin to look like a turkey.

"How are the boys progressing?" Rita winked at Grace and said under her breath, "Let the kids get it over with, so they can go and play."

After an argument with their mother over what to play, which Gladys won, or thought she did, they sat down to play a duet arrangement of "Amazing Grace."

I slipped to the kitchen to check the turkey. There I could listen to the boys while farther removed from the ceaseless pounding of Glady's voice explaining, explaining, explaining.

Albert came through the kitchen toward the back door.

"They're good, aren't they?" I said.

"They really are," he said with pride. "They're beginning to enjoy it." And then in his droll way he added, "They've found out duets drown out their mother's talking. They even practice theory in unison. Good for their timing, they say. Double volume too."

He stood with his hand on the doorknob, listening and smiling. I forgot he was there until he spoke again. "You look great, Ally. You been doing some soul puzzling?" The sadness in his voice swung me around. "Maybe you can answer one for me, Allison. What turns a green pasture by still waters into a waste, howling wilderness?"

"Beavers, Uncle Albert. Beavers." It was Mark on his way to catch his uncle enroute to the hockey nets. "Did you know that the sound of running water gives a beaver the urge to build a dam. When the dammed-up river floods good bushland, the foresters blast the dams apart and the water flows again. The beavers hear the flowing water and start building their dams again. Is that the right answer, Uncle Albert?"

"You're likely right, kid," Albert sighed. "A dam far enough back could turn a green valley into a waste, howling wilderness all right."

Randy and Danny brought their duet to a crescendo of final cords. Gladys went right on talking of her involvement in their music training, unaware that the boys had made their getaway to join their dad and cousins for some backyard competition at the hockey nets.

She carried right on through the dinner hour, but it wasn't unpleasant. Aunt Rita and Uncle Albert and the children carried on a two-level conversation among themselves. Randy and Danny had their father's wry humor and used it less discriminately. As long as their mother kept talking, they never paid any attention. When she showed signs of slowing, they listened until she set sail under full conversational canvas again.

On the whole, I felt the Thanksgiving dinner was a success. The food was good, the children well-behaved with each other, and mine helped with the work wonderfully.

Harvey seemed to enjoy it, as much as he ever does. He said his good-byes to everyone before leaving for work just before 4:00 P.M., his lunchbox packed with turkey sandwiches and pumpkin pie.

Soon after, Albert said his gracious-guest thank-yous, and the boys did the same.

Gladys looked me up and down. "It's a pity! You ate so little when you set such an excellent table. I do hope you'll cut out this fasting and dieting. It's just not good! When you've been plump, then lose a lot of weight, it makes you look so haggard and old."

"I'm glad you enjoyed the dinner." I accepted her left-handed compliment and ignored the right-handed punch she'd included. "It is good to get together like this. Time goes so fast, and the kids are growing up."

Then there was just Rita and the children. Rita was still helping, putting good china away, making turkey sandwiches for herself and the kids and me. She ran out to her car and brought back a big bottle of olives. "I just love olives with turkey and lettuce sandwiches. Since Harvey hates them, you never buy them, so I brought my own — enough for everybody!

"You make some coffee, Ally, and we'll celebrate all over again!"

With all the delight of forbidden fruit, we ate our supper — the kids watching a football game on TV and

Rita and I at the kitchen table, each with an extra kitchen
chair to prop up our tired feet.

Suddenly Rita set her coffee cup down and asked,
"What triggered it, Ally?"

Taken by surprise, I sputtered. Rita ate and waited in a
companionable, questioning silence.

So I told her. It was the first time I'd said it out loud
since Harvey convinced the pastor that it hadn't really
happened and I began writing to you, Joanna.

Hearing it again in my own voice, it seemed more like
a sad tale about a girl I used to know. The time since the
children were born, when my running began in earnest,
until now seems like a spin-off of the real me — that girl
with the horse, Captain, and the six six-foot uncles, and
Bible college, and church work, and the Christian wedding. . . .

Rita groaned, "Oh, my God! Thank the good Lord, He
called you back — " An explosion of cheers burst from the
living room. "For their sakes, as well as yours."

"Now you answer one for me, Rita. How come you're
so different from Gladys and Harvey?"

"I'm not quite sure what you mean. For instance?"

"For a starter, when Jeremy had scarlet fever."

She laughed. "That's the last time Harvey spoke a
civil word to me. I guess I really let him have it, didn't I?"

She certainly did, Joanna: "So, big brother, your idea
of being the helpful husband is *making yourself scarce?*
The truth is, even you, Harvey, haven't the nerve to expect
food and sex on demand from a girl working around the
clock with three children, one at death's door."

Harvey replied with his usual questioning: "You want
I should stay off work? Lose a day's pay? Two? With
medical bills? If you can afford to think so rich, you do it. If
you think Ally's all that bad off, you help her."

And she did, Joanna. Rita muttered to herself while
she waited for our party line to phone the school board for a

supply teacher — "He makes me sick to my stomach. He knows the price of everything and the value of nothing . . . nothing . . . nothing. A wife, a mother, a sick child, a soul has no price — so it has no value to Harvey either."

Joanna, Joanna, how I thank God that the cold, black waters of Georgian Bay shocked me into some sense, enough to struggle back to shore, back to my children, and to Him — who puts value on my soul.

I prompted Rita out of her pondering, "Gladys talks so. It doesn't seem to matter if anyone listens or not, and — "

"And Harvey is the same!"

"But, Rita, I can't get Harvey to talk!"

"Oh, no! You can't get him to listen. Any more than you can get Gladys to listen. Only with Harvey, he shuts you out with his attitude — 'This is the law around here. The master has spoken. This is a recording.' And snap goes the connection.

"Ally, seeing you as you are now, I'd say those letters to your friend Joanna have got to be the best story you've ever written — and more common than you think. I hear it over and over again, from kids whose parents are both unaware, and the kids are being pulled two directions at once and hanging on to their sanity by their fingernails."

"Rita, you didn't answer my question."

She chuckled a deep, throaty laugh. "I have my idiosyncrasies too, but I'm aware of them. You know the little lunacies that keep one level-headed.

"Like that Vette out there. One woman weighing all of 118 pounds does not need a 454-cubic-inch engine in her car — except to prove to Harvey and Gladys that muscle cars aren't masculine and that you don't have to be a man to own one. All it takes is money. It'll probably never wear out, so when I'm white-haired and frail you'll see a little, old lady still driving around in a white Vette." She laughed a happy throaty sound.

"Don't take that brother of mine so seriously. Albert and the kids don't let Gladys get them down. He's carved a niche of usefulness for himself. You do the same. With your talent —

"Maybe this sounds old-maidish to you, Allison, but all marriage has a margin of mutual misunderstanding in it. I've seen it over and over again among teachers. Take Albert for instance. He married a friendly, ambitious girl with Christian interests. He had no way of knowing that after marriage she'd turn into a super mother! Any more than you had any clue that Harvey would turn into the absentee father ruling by rote.

"What both my siblings need is a real honest-to-God dose of repentance. Remember the path of King Saul — anger — jealousy — an evil spirit."

Joanna, I guess I was shocked and showed it, for she went on.

"You'd do the Christian community a real service if you'd probe anger like you have obesity. I'll volunteer as your correspondent for that one. You might even help Harvey."

"Harvey would never read it, even if it was in print."

"No, not likely, but thousands of other angry Christians would."

At half-time of the television game, the children came out to the kitchen for refills on turkey sandwiches and pie. When Rita and I sat down for our second cup of coffee, it was still on Rita's mind.

"Ally, I was three years old when my mother left home. I went to that bus every day for the next week, and every day for the next month. Every day I expected her to come home, as she had left — on the bus between Hillsburg and Georgian Sound.

"God only knows the agony of expectation I suffered every time that bus pulled in, and the agony of disappointment every time it pulled out.

"I suffered in a terrible silence as I stood alone on that cracked sidewalk, breathing the fumes of the disappearing bus.

"Once that bus was out of sight, there was nothing silent about my suffering. I yelled and cried to my brother and my sister and my father and the church and anyone else who got in my way.

"One Mother's Day the Sunday school superintendent, who was given to patting little girls on the head, held out his hand to pat, muttering under his breath about irresponsible and loose women and my being better off with my father. I bit him. I bit until he yelped! Then I yelled the louder, 'I don't care what you think about her, *I want my mother!*'

"I was a terrible source of embarrassment to my father and Gladys and Harvey. But I suffered, as a child for its mother.

"Gladys and Harvey pretended they didn't. They used her going as a scapegoat for everything they didn't have, couldn't get, or wouldn't be. No mother in the home. What do you expect? Poor children!

"Gladys and Harvey are still suffering from an ache they don't even know is there. No matter how much lord and master Harvey acts to you, or how supermother Gladys is in her home, it will never be enough. For somehow when one suffers a neglect he won't admit is there, there is never enough."

Joanna, Albert had described it correctly — green pastures turned into a waste, howling wilderness, when the flow of real feelings is dammed up.

"Oh, Rita, I never knew. I thought your mother was dead."

"She is. I planned to look her up after I paid back my student loans, but she died in a plane crash in California my first year of teaching.

"A funeral parlor phoned from California to the village drugstore to see if someone would claim the body. So the whole village knew before we did.

"Dad said she'd never have come back to him alive, so he'd not bring her back dead. Let the state bury her."

Rita stood up and shook her sleek suit into its neatly pressed lines. "Ally, be real. You've got four great kids and yourself and talent. You've got a lot to give of real value — and God is no one's debtor.

"This is the best Thanksgiving I've ever had. Thanks, Ally."

"You worked like a horse," I exclaimed.

"And so did you, and we both enjoyed it like free souls." She hugged me as a long-absent sister would, kissed Grace, shook hands with the boys, and promised them all souvenirs from Switzerland where she was chaperoning a group of students at the Christmas break.

With a loud purring in the driveway, she was gone.

I sat at the kitchen table for a while, staring into my empty coffee mug, thinking of the day and what she'd told me and of her offer to be my correspondent — *Love, Honor, and Anger.* Maybe such a manuscript would help me understand Harvey's problem, just as *Love, Honor, and Obesity* has helped me understand my unreal reasons for overeating.

On the strength of God's promise — "If any of you lack wisdom, let him ask of God" — I'd fought my way back from the nether world where I'd been trapped alone, somewhere between Harvey's irrational demands and my impossible dream.

Who am I to limit God?

His love has no limit, His grace has no measure,
His power no boundary known unto men.

A groan of agony shook the living room and was expelled in a few more minutes by a scream of delight. Mark shot straight up in the air, Jeremy sprung upright onto his feet, Grace looked up from her book to watch the replay, and Andrew slept on unseeing as the others gloried in the winning touchdown a second time.

Joanna, it was a wonderful Thanksgiving. I have so much I am thankful for as I watch these thinking, feeling, worshiping children in a happy moment of spectator play.

They scattered to the bathroom and refrigerator, paused to say their good-nights and to catch the TV commentator's last words on the game.

Jeremy noticed Andrew, picked him up, and carried him, still sleeping, to bed.

I stood alone in the living room — alone in the suddenly silent house, as I so often am. And I thought of all the times Harvey has snapped a pet put-down at me — "Why should you be lonely? You got the kids."

When reaching to him for some friendship, those words had stung with disappointment and discouragement — but neither of us knew how prophetic they were.

Joanna, I am *not* alone. How could one be alone with four thinking, feeling, worshiping beings?

Oh, they criticize each other, and compete with each other, and defend one against the other during the day. But come evening, they gather together against the night — these aware and caring kids.

I am no longer alone.

It is enough.

Your sister, the late arrival to adulthood,
Allison

Chapter 18

La Paz, Bolivia
Friday, November 15

Dear Allison,

All that made your Canadian Thanksgiving so good to you will be part of the thankfulness of mine, as we celebrate the American Thanksgiving next week here, high up in the Andes.

The altitude is a shock, but great for arthritis.

At the risk of sounding like the cynical old lady you once thought me to be — Remember, Allison, the urge to build an ivory tower has no age barrier. Continue to be alert and aware daily, for Satan has many disguises.

"If you love enough. . . ." Allison, you may yet prove that old adage to be applicable.

If one loves enough. Not the love that is sex on demand, or obedience with food on demand, or honoring that must do as I say and don't ask any questions — but the love of 1 Corinthians 13. Not the love that is a sounding brass, a bonging of a gong to call a slave to appear and serve — but the love that puts away childish things — childish dreams and disappointments, childish fears and angers — to become adult.

Rita's right. Our correspondence does have a story. For the Lord does fill the hungry with good things (Luke 1:53). There is a satisfied hunger without added calories when the spiritual dimension of one's being is alive and growing.

Once you stopped being what you were not in order to get what did not exist, you were filled to overflowing — but not obese.

That story deserves print. Is it a *Christian* story?

Love,

Joanna

Shale Bay, Ontario
Friday, November 22

Dear Joanna,
Best wishes for a good Thanksgiving.
I am not much for labels any more. The Balm of Gilead by any other name is still the Balm of Gilead.

Lovingly,

Allison

La Paz, Bolivia
Sunday, December 8

Dear Allison,
That's what I went to that conference, all of nine years ago, to find out.
A blessed Christmas for you all.

Love,

Joanna